POWER UP
KOREAN
VOCABULARY

POWER UP KOREAN VOCABULARY

Sang-Seok Yoon • Insung Ko

KOREA
UNIVERSITY
PRESS

SANG-SEOK YOON, PH.D. IS TEACHING KOREAN LANGUAGE AND LINGUISTICS AT THE UNIVERSITY OF IOWA.

INSUNG KO, PH.D. IS TEACHING KOREAN LANGUAGE AND LINGUISTICS AT THE GEORGE WASHINGTON UNIVERSITY.

KOREA UNIVERSITY PRESS
82-2-3290-4230 (TEL.) 82-2-923-6311 (FAX)
HTTP://WWW.KUPRESS.COM KUPRESS@KOREA.AC.KR
145, ANAM-RO, SEONGBUK-GU, SEOUL, 02841 KOREA

PUBLISHED 2015

ISBN: 978-89-7641-879-1

PRINTED IN REPUBLIC OF KOREA

Contents

Contents

Preface

Foreign language educators and learners will agree that vocabulary acquisition is the most important component for a student to advance to a higher level. Vocabulary acquisition is especially essential for beginning-level students because their understanding of grammatical structure is still basic. However, vocabulary learning requires a great deal of effort and time, often accompanied by tedious recitation or writing words many times. Korean vocabulary is especially hard to learn because there are so many words with similar sounds and spellings. There are many homonyms and synonyms, and even slight changes in consonants (e.g. ㅈ and ㅊ, ㄱ and ㅋ) and vowels (ㅗ and ㅓ, ㅐ and ㅔ) with similar pronunciations often result in totally different meanings. Also, simple translations from Korean into English are not sufficient for a student to grasp the exact meaning of a word because understanding a word should be supported by etymological and cultural knowledge. Therefore, many have given up learning Korean in their beginning level and failed to advance to a higher level.

This book is designed for beginning-level Korean learners who want to solidify their foundation of Korean by enlarging their vocabulary in order to have more confidence using Korean. This book is ideal for the following students:

- Students who are in a beginning-level Korean class.
- Students who are in an intermediate-level class, but are often still confused when using basic words.
- Students who are preparing for the TOPIK (Test of Proficiency in Korean).
- Students who have studied Korean for a while and want to solidify their foundational knowledge of Korean.

PREFACE

This book is not a simple Korean-English glossary, but rather provides much richer essential information for understanding words along with their variations in collocations. This book presents 500 essential words, with an emphasis on those most commonly used in beginning-level textbooks and the TOPIK beginning-level vocabulary list. We grouped 20 random words in each unit, which learners can study at one time without too much effort. When vocabulary acquisition takes place, learners achieve multiple layers of lexical information that consists of the association between forms and meanings. Thus the most common meanings and usages of each word in this book's 25 lessons are accompanied by example sentences, grammatical information, cultural information, and related words as well as morphophonemic information, such as Chinese origin, pronunciation, and conjugation patterns. This book offers further helpful advice about the most common mistakes we have encountered in student work.

While using this book, students' acquired knowledge of meanings and usages of essential basic words will help them communicate more effectively with Korean people and succeed in school as well as on standardized tests. Consequently, students are expected to feel more confident in Korean language and culture and continue studying at a higher level.

The unique characteristics of this book highlight the following:

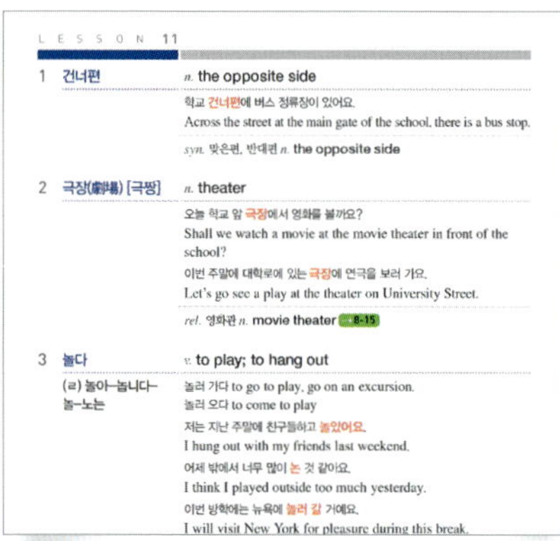
LESSON 11

1 건너편 — *n.* the opposite side
학교 건너편에 버스 정류장이 있어요.
Across the street at the main gate of the school, there is a bus stop.
syn. 맞은편, 반대편 *n.* the opposite side

2 극장(劇場) [극짱] — *n.* theater
오늘 학교 앞 극장에서 영화를 볼까요?
Shall we watch a movie at the movie theater in front of the school?
이번 주말에 대학로에 있는 극장에 연극을 보러 가요.
Let's go see a play at the theater on University Street.
rel. 영화관 *n.* movie theater 8-15

3 놀다 — *v.* to play; to hang out
(ㄹ) 놀아–놉니다–놀–노는
놀러 가다 to go to play, go on an excursion.
놀러 오다 to come to play
저는 지난 주말에 친구들하고 놀았어요.
I hung out with my friends last weekend.
어제 밖에서 너무 많이 논 것 같아요.
I think I played outside too much yesterday.
이번 방학에는 뉴욕에 놀러 갈 거예요.
I will visit New York for pleasure during this break.

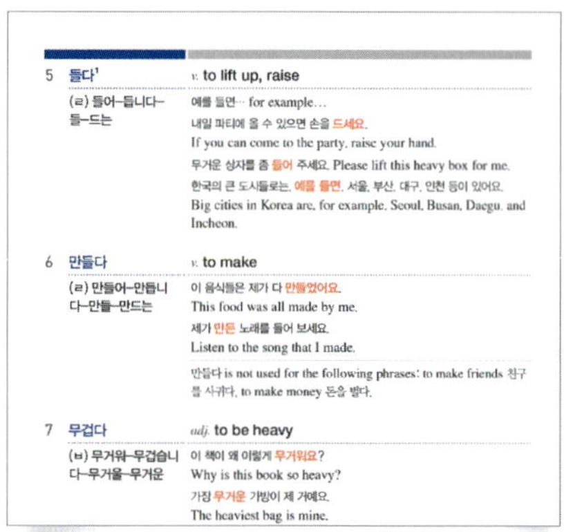
5 들다[1] — *v.* to lift up, raise
(ㄹ) 들어–듭니다–들–드는
예를 들면… for example…
내일 파티에 올 수 있으면 손을 드세요.
If you can come to the party, raise your hand.
무거운 상자를 좀 들어 주세요. Please lift this heavy box for me.
한국의 큰 도시들로는, 예를 들면, 서울, 부산, 대구, 인천 등이 있어요.
Big cities in Korea are, for example, Seoul, Busan, Daegu, and Incheon.

6 만들다 — *v.* to make
(ㄹ) 만들어–만듭니다–만들–만드는
이 음식들은 제가 다 만들었어요.
This food was all made by me.
제가 만든 노래를 들어 보세요.
Listen to the song that I made.
만들다 is not used for the following phrases: to make friends 친구를 사귀다, to make money 돈을 벌다.

7 무겁다 — *adj.* to be heavy
(ㅂ) 무거워–무겁습니다–무거울–무거운
이 책이 왜 이렇게 무거워요?
Why is this book so heavy?
가장 무거운 가방이 제 거예요.
The heaviest bag is mine.

- For all entry words in the text, typological enhancement in color, **bold** and/or *italicized* fonts is added in order to draw the reader's attention more effectively.
- For Sino-Korean words, Chinese characters are provided for those who understand them. This inclusion also helps learners understand what meaningful elements compose each word (e.g. 간식 [間食]).
- Pronunciations are provided when the word is not spoken exactly as it is written (e.g. 같이 [가치]).
- For irregular verbs and adjectives, four basic conjugation forms that demonstrate conjugational patterns are provided (e.g. (ㅂ) 가까워—가깝습니다—가까울—가까운). See below for more details.
- Important grammatical information is provided that takes into consideration errors commonly found in learners' writing and speaking (e.g. 결혼하다 cannot take a direct object: the basic structure is "person 하고 결혼(을) 하다 to marry person").
- When a word has several meanings, we selected the most representative meanings that are frequently used at the beginning level.
- Essential derivatives and compound forms are listed under the entry words (e.g. 결혼: 결혼하다, 결혼식).
- Commonly used phrasal expressions are also provided (e.g. 약 'medicine' —약을 먹다 'to take medicine', 약을 바르다 'to apply medicine').
- Synonyms (*syn.*), antonyms (*ant.*), and related words (*rel.*) are given so that students can understand the meaning clearly and expand their vocabulary in comparison to other related words (e.g. 입원 *ant.* 퇴원, 잠깐 *syn.* 잠시).
- Simple but helpful pedagogical tips are given concerning frequent mistakes made by Korean learners. Commonly used colloquial forms are provided for students' better understanding (예쁘다—이쁘다).
- In addition to simple exercises after each chapter, various types of review exercises are provided for self-assessment.
- The appendix presents some essential words with pictures that enhance students' ability to memorize them by visualizing those words in meaningful contexts.

- The glossary contains all the entry words as well as the other words that appear in the explanation or antonym, synonym, and related words sections. Related lessons and entry numbers are indicated or cross-referenced for students' convenience.

Irregular types of verbs and adjectives

Korean verbs and adjectives may be conjugated into various forms depending on the phonological condition between the verbal stem and the grammatical suffix. Roughly speaking, grammatical suffixes can be categorized into three patterns: consonant-beginning suffixes such as +고 or +네, (으)-beginning suffixes such as +(으)면 or +(으)러, and (어/아)-beginning suffixes such as +어/아요 or +었/았.

When Korean verbs and adjectives associate with these suffixes, they follow lexically inherent conjugation types, which can be regular or irregular. In particular, some irregular adjectives and verbs show typical patterns in conjugation, depending on the consonant or vowel that their stem ends with, as follows:

- (ㄹ) ㄹ–deletion (e.g., 날다, 살다, 알다) The stem-final consonant ㄹ drops when it is followed by (으) beginning suffix, as in 살다 –살면. It also drops when it is followed by ㅂ, ㄴ, ㅅ-beginning suffixes, such as –ㅂ니다, –네요, –는, –세요 as in 살다 – 삽니다, 사네요, 사는, 사세요. When the suffix contains ㄹ, as in–(으)ㄹ, only one ㄹ is articulated in the surface form, as in 살다 – 살 거예요, 살래요.
- (으) 으–deletion (e.g., 나쁘다, 아프다, 예쁘다) The stem final vowel–drops when it is followed by vowel-beginning suffixes, such as –(으)면, –(어/아)요 as in 예쁘다 – 예쁘면, 예뻐요.
- (ㄷ) ㄷ–irregular (e.g., 걷다, 듣다, 묻다) The stem final ㄷ changes to ㄹ when it is followed by vowel-beginning suffixes, as in 걷다 – 걸으면, 걸어요.
- (르) 르–irregular (e.g., 다르다, 모르다, 부르다) The stem-final 르 changes to double ㄹ at the stem-final and suffix-initial positions when it is followed by (어/아)– beginning suffixes, as in 다르다 – 달라요, 달라서.

- (ㅂ) ㅂ-irregular (e.g., 덥다, 돕다, 춥다) The stem-final ㅂ changes to 우 when it is followed by vowel-beginning suffixes, as in 춥다 – 추우면, 추워요. The ㅂ changes to 오 instead of 우 for two monosyllabic words, 돕다 and 곱다, when it is followed by (어/아)– beginning suffixes, as in – 도와요, 고와요 but 도우면, 고우면, respectively.
- (ㅅ) ㅅ–irregular (e.g., 낫다, 잇다, 짓다) The stem-final ㅅ drops when it is followed by vowel-beginning suffixes, as in 낫다 – 나은, 나으면, 나았어요.
- (ㅎ) ㅎ–irregular (e.g., 그렇다, 빨갛다, 하얗다) The stem final ㅎ drops when it is followed by (으)–beginning suffixes, as in 하얗다 – 하얀, 하야면. When it is followed by (어/ 아) beginning suffixes, the stem ㅎ drops and the following vowel is shifted to be a front vowel, as in 하얗다 – 하얘요, 하얘서.

Thus, this book presents four representative conjugational forms of irregular verbs and adjectives that beginners in learning Korean are likely to make errors with. The first one is the (어/아)요 'informal polite form' which represents –(어/아) beginning suffixes, such as, –(어/아)서 'because, as', or –(어/아)ㅆ 'past suffix'. The second one is the formal polite (or deferential) form –(스)ㅂ니다. The 스 should drop when the preceding stem ends with a vowel. It also drops the preceding ㄹ of ㄹ–deletion words. The third form shows how the word changes when it is followed by (으)–beginning suffixes represented by the form of –(으)ㄹ 'future suffix' for –(으)면 'if', –(으)러 'in order to', or –(으)시– 'subject honorific suffix', and so on. The fourth form shows the present tense noun modifying form, which distinguishes verbs in –는 from adjectives in –(으)ㄴ; for instance 가다 'to go' – 가는, 살다 'to live' – 사는 in comparison with 예쁘다 'to be pretty' – 예쁜, 작다 'to be small' – 작은.

Abbreviations

adj. adjective
adv. adverb
ant. antonym
n. noun
rel. related word(s), words that are good to study with the entry words
syn. synonym
v. verb

Acknowledgments

We have benefited from the insightful comments and suggestions of several people during our preparation of this book. First of all, we would like to express our gratitude to Prof. Seok-Hoon You for having encouraged us to develop and publish this book. Without his help, our project couldn't have been completed. We are also grateful to Hae-joo Yoon and Irene Ko for making the English translations easily understandable for readers. We also thank Margie Gomez, Brittany Flook, Ananya Kumar, and Ethan Ko for their valuable feedback after reading and completing exercises in previous drafts of this work. Our special thanks to our illustrator, Jung Min Son, and the staff at Korea University Press for editing this book beautifully.

LESSON 01

1 **가게** *n.* **store; shop**

옷 가게 clothing store, 신발 가게 shoe store, 선물 가게 gift shop, 화장품 가게 cosmetics store

이 **가게**에서는 예쁜 옷을 팔아요. This store sells beautiful clothes.

syn. 상점 *n.* **store, shop** →2-11

2 **괜찮다 [괜찬타]** *adj.* **to be okay**

학교 식당 음식이 **괜찮아요**?
Is the food at the school restaurant okay?

몸은 좀 **괜찮아요**? Are you feeling okay?

괜찮다 literally means 'not very bad', so it should not be used for describing something really good.

3 **나쁘다** *adj.* **to be bad**

(—) 나빠–나쁩니다–나쁠–나쁜

나빠지다 to get worse, 기분이 나쁘다 to feel bad

담배는 건강에 **나빠요**. Smoking is bad for your health.

이번 주에는 날씨가 점점 **나빠지고** 있어요.
The weather is getting worse this week.

ant. 좋다 *adj.* **to be good** →3-18

4 **달리다** *v.* **to run, dash**

달리기 running

저는 100미터 **달리기**에서 1등을 했어요.
I won first place in the 100-meter race.

자동차를 너무 빨리 **달리지** 마세요. Don't drive your car too fast.

달리다 can be used to describe the movement of people, animals or cars, while 뛰다 'to run, hop, jump' is generally used for people or animals with feet. →24-5

5 **돌려주다** *v.* **to return (something)**

어제 친구한테 책을 빌렸어요. 내일 **돌려줄 거예요**. I borrowed a book from my friend yesterday. I will return it tomorrow.

The humble form of 돌려주다 is 돌려 드리다 'to return (something to a socially higher person)'.

이 책은 선생님께 **돌려 드려야** 해요.

I have to return this book to my teacher.

6 뜻 *n.* **meaning, sense**

선생님, 이 단어의 **뜻**이 뭐예요?

Teacher, what is the meaning of this word?

이 문장은 무슨 **뜻**인지 모르겠어요.

I don't know what this sentence means.

7 며칠 *n.* **what day of the month; a few days**

오늘이 몇 월 **며칠**이에요? What is the month and date today?

여름 방학까지 **며칠** 남았어요?

How many days are left until the summer vacation?

Note that 몇일 is not a correct spelling.

8 바꾸다 *v.* **to switch, change**

바뀌다 *v.* to be changed

저하고 자리를 **바꿀래요**? Would you like to change seats with me?

김 교수님 좀 **바꿔** 주시겠어요?

Can you put Prof. Kim on the phone?

벌써 계절이 **바뀌었어요**. The season has (been) changed already.

9 벽(壁) *n.* **wall**

벽시계 a (wall) clock, 벽화 mural

벽에 그림을 하나 걸고 싶어요. I want to hang a picture on the wall.

현우는 거실 **벽**을 파란색으로 칠했어요.

Hyeonwu painted the living room walls blue.

10 비밀(秘密) *n.* **secret**

비밀을 지키다 to keep a secret

저하고 제 남자 친구는 서로 **비밀**이 없어요.

My boyfriend and I do not have any secrets with each other.

오늘 제가 한 얘기는 **비밀**이에요. What I told you today is a secret.

11 **상처(傷處)** *n.* **injury, wound, cut**

상처가 생기다 to be wounded, hurt

축구를 하다가 넘어져서 무릎에 **상처가 생겼어요.**

I got injured on my knee because I fell while playing soccer.

이 **상처**에는 매일 연고를 발라야 해요.

You have to put ointment on this cut every day.

12 **소리** *n.* **sound**

목소리 voice, 소리를 지르다 to scream, shout

밖에서 이상한 **소리**가 들려요.

I can hear a strange sound from outside.

13 **시청(市廳)** *n.* **city hall**

토요일 2시에 (서울) **시청** 앞에서 만나자.

Let's meet in front of the (Seoul) City Hall at 2:00 PM on Saturday.

14 **씻다** *v.* **to wash**

손을 자주 **씻으면** 감기에 안 걸릴 거예요.

If you wash your hands often, you will not catch a cold.

이 과일들을 잘 **씻어서** 드세요.

Wash these fruits before you eat them.

15 **연구실(研究室)** *n.* **professor's office; laboratory**

교수님, 질문이 하나 있는데, 교수님 **연구실**로 가도 돼요?

Professor, I have a question. Can I stop by your office?

저는 생화학 **연구실**에서 일해요.

I work for the laboratory of Biochemistry.

rel. 실험실 *n.* **laboratory, lab**, 사무실 *n.* **office**

16 **웬일 [웬닐]** *n.* **what matter...? what reason...?**

가: 김 선생님, 공항에는 **웬일**이세요?
Mr. Kim, what brings you to the airport?

나: 오늘 제 친구가 와요. My friend is coming today.

Be careful not to confuse 웬 in 웬일 with 왠 in 왠지 'for some reason' or 왜 'why'.

17 **자다** *v.* to sleep
잠 *n.* sleep

잠(을) 자다 to sleep, 잠이 들다 to fall asleep, 잠이 오다 to get sleepy

시험 때문에 **잠**을 못 **잤어요**. 이번 주말에는 **잠**을 푹 **자고** 싶어요.
I couldn't sleep because of exams. This weekend, I want to sleep deeply.

내일 중요한 발표가 있어서 오늘 **잠**을 못 **잘** 것 같다.
Since I have an important presentation tomorrow, I don't think I will be able to sleep tonight.

rel. 주무시다 *v.* to sleep (honorific)
우리 할머니는 일찍 **주무시고** 일찍 일어나세요.
My grandmother goes to sleep early and wakes up early.

18 **종업원(從業員)** *n.* waiter, waitress; employee

그 식당은 음식은 맛있는데 **종업원**이 별로 안 친절해요.
The restaurant serves good food but the waitresses are not very friendly.

19 **찍다** *v.* to take (a photograph), film (a video/movie)

저는 여행 가서 사진을 많이 **찍었어요**.
I took many pictures on the trip.
이 영화는 부산에서 **찍었어요**. This movie was filmed in Busan.

20 **편하다(便–)** *adj.* to be comfortable; to feel easy

신발이 아주 가볍고 **편하네요**.
These shoes are very light and comfortable!
마음이 **편하면** 몸도 **편해요**.
When the mind is at ease, so is your body.

편하다 vs. 편리하다 ···› 24-18
편하다 generally means something feels physically or mentally comfortable, while 편리하다 is something is convenient to use (*e.g.* 서울은 교통이 편리해요. The transportation in Seoul is convenient.)

syn. 편안하다 *adj.* to be comfortable *ant.* 불편하다 *adj.* to be uncomfortable; to be inconvenient ···› 21-9

CHECK UP

가게, 며칠, 벽, 상처, 시청, 연구실, 뜻, 비밀, 소리, 종업원, 웬일

1 city hall ______

2 injury, wound, cut ______

3 professor's office; laboratory ______

4 store; shop ______

5 meaning, sense ______

6 secret ______

7 sound ______

8 waiter, waitress; employee ______

9 wall ______

10 what day of the month; a few days ______

11 what matter...? ______

CHECK UP

괜찮다, 달리다, 바꾸다, 씻다, 편하다, 나쁘다, 돌려주다, 자다, 찍다

1 to be comfortable ______________________

2 to be okay ______________________

3 to run, dash ______________________

4 to switch, change ______________________

5 to wash ______________________

6 to be bad ______________________

7 to return (something) ______________________

8 to sleep ______________________

9 to take (a photograph), film (a movie) ______________________

English loanwords exercise 1:

The following words are English loanwords used in Korea.
Write an equivalent English word next to each word.

1 게임 ....
2 달러 ....
3 데이트 ....
4 디지털 카메라 ....
5 러시아워 ....
6 비타민 ....
7 빌딩 ....
8 샤워 ....
9 세일 ....
10 소파 ....
11 쇼핑 ....
12 스트레스 ....
13 이메일 ....
14 인터넷 ....
15 인터뷰 ....
16 카드 ....
17 캠퍼스 ....
18 컵 ....
19 코미디 ....
20 코트 ....
21 콘서트 ....
22 택시 ....
23 테이블 ....
24 텔레비전 ....
25 트럭 ....
26 패션 ....
27 팩스 ....
28 헤드폰 ....
29 호텔 ....
30 홈페이지 ....

Answer

1 game **2** dollar **3** date **5** digital camera **5** rush hour **6** vitamin **7** building **8** shower **9** sale **10** sofa **11** shopping **12** stress **13** email **14** internet **15** interview **16** card **17** campus **18** cup **19** comedy **20** coat **21** concert **22** taxi **23** table **24** television **25** truck **26** fashion **27** fax **28** headphones **29** hotel **30** homepage

LESSON 02

1 **가깝다** *adj.* **to be close**

(ㅂ) 가까워–
가깝습니다–
가까울–가까운

가까운 집 close house, 가까운 친구 close friends

집이 학교에서 **가까워요**. My house is close to school.

나하고 **가까운** 친구들은 다 제 고향에 살고 있어요.
All close friends of mine are living in my hometown.

ant. 멀다 *adj.* **to be far** → 23-7

2 **굉장히** *adv.* **very; extremely**
굉장하다 *adj.* **to be amazing, magnificent**

저 영화는 **굉장히** 재미있어요. That movie is extremely entertaining.

1980년대 마이클 잭슨의 인기는 정말 **굉장했어요**.
In the 1980s, Michael Jackson was tremendously popular.

syn. 아주 → 6-14, 매우 → 18-6 *adv.* **very much**; 대단히, 굉장히
adv. **greatly, extremely**

3 **나이** *n.* **age**

나이가 많다 to be old, 나이가 적다/어리다 to be young

나이가 어떻게 되세요? (=몇 살이에요?) How old are you?

저는 (**나이**가) 스무 살이에요. I am 20 years old.

For talking about a senior's age, honorific word "연세" should be used. **연세**가 어떻게 되세요? What is your age?

syn. 연세 *n.* **age (honorific)**

4 **닮다 [담따]** *v.* **to resemble, take after, look alike**

닮은 [달믄] looking alike

저는 엄마를 **닮았어요**. I resemble my mother.

어제 저는 제가 좋아하는 배우를 **닮은** 사람을 봤어요.
Yesterday, I saw a person who looks like my favorite actor.

Note that this is a verb and the resultative form "닮았다" should be used for describing the current state. Thus, "저는 엄마를 닮아요." is not a natural sentence.

5 **돕다** *v.* **to help**
도움 *n.* **help**

(ㅂ) 도와–돕습니다–도울–돕는

도와주다/도와 드리다 to give/lend help

저는 어머니가 요리하는 것을 도와 드렸어요. I helped my mother cook.

도와주세요. Help me!

6 마르다[1]

v. to dry up

(르) 말라–마릅니다–마를–마르는

오늘은 바람이 불어서 빨래가 잘 마를 거예요.
It is windy today, so my laundry will dry very well.

rel. 말리다 *v.* to dry something

7 면도(面刀)
면도하다

n. shaving
v. to shave

면도기 razor

노아는 아침에 면도를 해도 오후가 되면 수염이 또 자라요.
Even though Noah shaves in the morning, by afternoon his facial hair grows back.

rel. 수염 *n.* facial hair, 턱수염 *n.* beard, 콧수염 *n.* mustache

8 바다

n. sea, ocean

바닷가 seaside, beach

이 바다 밑에는 예쁜 물고기들이 많이 있어요.
There are many beautiful fish under this sea.

rel. 산 *n.* mountain, 강 *n.* river, 호수 *n.* lake

9 별

n. star

오늘은 하늘이 맑아서 별이 많이 보여요.
The sky is clear, so many stars can be seen.

10 비슷하다 [비스타다]

adj. to be similar, alike

저하고 제 남동생은 키가 비슷해요.
My younger brother and I are similar in height.

저는 어머니하고 비슷한 성격이에요.
My mother and I have similar personalities.

rel. (똑)같다, *adj.* to be (exactly) same → 9-1

11 **상점(商店)** *v.* **store, shop**

저 **상점**에는 정말 다양한 물건들이 있어요. That store carries various kinds of items.

syn. 가게 *n.* store ⋯ 1-1

12 **소설(小說)** *n.* **novel, fiction**

소설가 *n.* novelist

어떤 **소설**을 좋아하세요? What kind of novels do you enjoy?

저는 **소설가**가 되고 싶어요. I want to become a novelist.

rel. 시 *n.* poetry, poem

13 **시키다** *v.* **to order (food in a restaurant); to make someone do something**

제가 조금 늦을 것 같아요. 저 기다리지 말고 먼저 음식을 **시키세요**.
I think I'll be a little late. Please don't wait for me and order your meal.

저한테 노래를 **시키지** 마세요. Please don't ask me to sing.

syn. 주문하다 *v.* to place an order ⋯ 7-18

14 **아까** *adv.* **a while ago**

가: 현우 여기 있어요? Is Hyeonwu here?

나: 아니요. **아까** 기숙사로 갔어요.
No. He left for the dorm a while ago.

ant. 이따가 *adv.* after a while

15 **연락(連絡) [열락]** *n.* **contact**
연락하다 [열라카다] *v.* **to contact**

연락처 *n.* contact information (*e.g.* phone number, e-mail address)

부모님께는 얼마나 자주 **연락하세요**?
How often do you contact your parents?

연락처가 어떻게 되세요? What is your contact information?

16 유명하다(有名–) *adj.* **to be famous**

이 한국 식당에서는 비빔밥이 **유명해요**.
At this Korean restaurant, *bibimbap* is famous.
이번 공연에서는 **유명한** 가수들을 많이 볼 수 있어요.
At this concert, you can see many famous singers.

…(으)로 유명하다 to be famous for…
이 식당은 비빔밥으로 **유명합니다**.
This restaurant is famous for its *bibimbap*.

17 자동차(自動車) *n.* **car, automobile**

우리 집에서 학교까지 **자동차**로 15분 걸려요.
From my house to school, it takes 15 minutes by car.

자동 means "automatic" and found in words like 자동문 'automatic door', and 자동판매기 'vending machine'.

syn. 차 *n.* **car**

18 종이 *n.* **(a piece of) paper**

프린터에 **종이**가 없어요. There is no paper in the printer.
요즘 많은 슈퍼에서는 **종이** 가방에 물건을 넣어 줘요.
These days, many supermarkets give products in paper bags.

For counting papers, 장 is used for a counter.
종이 한 장만 주세요. Please give me a piece of paper.

19 차다 *v.* **to kick**

그 공 좀 이쪽으로 **차** 주세요. Please kick the ball this way.

You can kick a ball (공을 차다) but you cannot kick soccer. So, 축구를 차다 is a wrong phrase but you should say 축구를 하다 'to play soccer'. Likewise, you can hit a baseball (야구공을 치다) but you cannot hit a baseball game. So, 야구를 치다 is a wrong phrase but you should say 야구를 하다 'to play baseball'.

20 평일(平日) *n.* **weekday**

평일에는 이 공원에 사람들이 별로 없는데, 오늘은 토요일이라서 사람이 많네요. There are not many people at this park on weekdays, but since today is Saturday, there are many people.

rel. 주말 *n.* **weekend** → 6-18

CHECK UP

나이, 면도, 별, 상점, 아까, 자동차, 소설, 종이, 평일, 바다

1 a while ago ______________________

2 age ______________________

3 car ______________________

4 shaving ______________________

5 star ______________________

6 novel ______________________

7 paper ______________________

8 sea, ocean ______________________

9 weekday ______________________

10 store, shop ______________________

CHECK UP

괭장하다, 닮다, 마르다, 비슷하다, 연락하다, 유명하다,
차다, 가깝다, 돕다, 시키다

1 to be close ______

2 to help ______

3 to kick ______

4 to be amazing, magnificent ______

5 to be famous ______

6 to be similar ______

7 to dry up ______

8 to resemble ______

9 to order (food),
to ask someone to do... ______

10 to contact ______

English loanwords exercise 2:

The following words are English loanwords used in Korea.
Write an equivalent English word next to each word.

1	뉴스	________	16	커튼	________
2	드라마	________	17	커피	________
3	라디오	________	18	컴퓨터	________
4	바나나	________	19	콜라	________
5	버스	________	20	클래스	________
6	비디오	________	21	토크 쇼	________
7	비즈니스	________	22	트럭	________
8	샐러드	________	23	티셔츠	________
9	서비스	________	24	팝송	________
10	오렌지	________	25	패스트 푸드	________
11	온라인	________	26	프레젠테이션	________
12	와인	________	27	플라스틱	________
13	재즈	________	28	피자	________
14	초콜릿	________	29	햄버거	________
15	치즈	________	30	힙합	________

Answer

1 news **2** drama **3** radio **4** banana **5** bus **6** video **7** business **8** salad **9** service **10** orange **11** online **12** wine **13** jazz **14** chocolate **15** cheese **16** curtain **17** coffee **18** computer **19** cola **20** class **21** talk show **22** truck **23** t-shirt **24** pop song **25** fast food **26** presentation **27** plastic **28** pizza **29** hamburger **30** hip hop

LESSON 03

1 **가끔** *adv.* **sometimes, once in a while, occasionally**

저는 가끔 운동을 해요. 아마 한 달에 한두 번쯤 할 거예요.
I exercise once in a while: probably once or twice a month.

rel. 자주 *adv.* **often** →5-17

2 **교과서(教科書)** *n.* **textbook**

여러분, 교과서를 펴세요. Everyone, open your textbook.

3 **날씨** *n.* **weather**

날씨가 좋다/나쁘다. The weather is good/bad.
내일은 날씨가 추워질 거예요.
The weather is going to get colder tomorrow.

rel. 일기예보 *n.* **weather forecast** →16-16

4 **담그다** *v.* **to soak, put something in liquid; to make (kimchi)**

(—) 담가-담급니다-담글-담그는

물에 손을 담갔어요. I soaked my hands in water.
저는 엄마한테 김치 담그는 법을 배웠어요.
I learned how to make kimchi from my mother.

Be careful not to spell it as 담궈요 or 담거요 as you may hear often in colloquial speech.

5 **동네** *n.* **village, town; neighborhood area**

동네 사람 neighborhood people (= 이웃)
우리는 같은 동네에 살아요. We live in the same neighborhood.
우리 동네 사람들은 참 친절해요.
Our neighborhood people are very friendly.

6 **먹다** *v.* **to eat (food); to drink (liquid); to take (medicine)**

밥을 먹다 to eat a meal, 약을 먹다 to take medicine
술을 먹다 to drink alcohol, 나이를 먹다 to get old
점심에 뭐 먹을까요? What shall we eat for lunch?

Note that we can say 아침/점심/저녁을 먹다, while we don't say 식사를 먹다, but must say 식사를 하다. →6-13

rel. 마시다 *v.* **to drink** →4-6

7 **모두** *n./adv.* **all, all together**

모두 얼마예요? How much is all together?

우리 가족은 아버지, 어머니, 언니 한 명, 남동생 한 명 그리고 저, **모두** 다섯 명이에요. In my family, there are my father, mother, older sister, younger brother, and me, five people in total.

저는 이번 달 월급을 **모두** 써 버려서 돈이 하나도 없어요.
This month, I used up all of my salary, so I have no money left.

syn. 전부 *n./adv.* all, the entire

8 **바라다** *v.* **to wish, want, hope**

다시 만나기를 간절히 **바랍니다**. I sincerely wish to see you again.

저는 돈을 **바라고** 일하지 않았습니다. I didn't work for the money.

The polite informal form of 바라다 should be 바라요, but many Korean speakers are likely to use 바래요, in colloquial speech. In this sense, its noun form is 바람 while, colloquially, 바램, a wrong form, is often used. 내 **바람**은 좋은 여자 친구를 만나는 것이에요. My wish is to meet a good girlfriend.

syn. 원하다 *v.* to want, ~고 싶다 *adj.* to want to~, would like to ~

9 **별로** *adv.* **(not) really, (not) particularly**

오늘은 **별로** 안 바빠요. I am not very busy today.

우리 엄마가 한 음식은 사실 **별로** 맛이 없어요. The food my mom cooks is actually not very delicious.

As shown in the examples, 별로 should be followed by a negative expression or a word with negative meaning.

10 **비싸다** *adj.* **to be expensive**

한국에서는 수박이 아주 **비싸요**.
In Korea, watermelons are very expensive.

어제 백화점에서 **비싼** 옷을 샀어요.
Yesterday, I bought expensive clothes at the department store.

ant. 싸다 *adj.* to be cheap → 18-13

11 **새로** — *adv.* **newly**

현우는 **새로** 산 바지가 너무 작아서 바꾸려고 해요.
Hyeonwu's newly bought pants are too small, so he is intending to exchange them.

소현이는 다음 주부터 **새로** 아르바이트를 시작해요.
Sohyeon starts a new part-time job starting next week.

rel. 새 *adj.* **new**

12 **소식(消息)** — *n.* **news**

고등학교 때 친구들 **소식**은 자주 들어요?
Do you often hear about friends from high school?

This word 소식 is used only for news in interpersonal relationships. Koreans use a loanword 뉴스 for the news from the media such as a newspaper or TV.

13 **시험(試驗)** — *n.* **test, exam**

단어 시험 vocabulary quiz

시험을 보다 *v.* to take an exam

공부를 열심히 해서 **시험**을 아주 잘 **봤어요**.
Because I studied hard, I did very well on the test.

14 **아름답다** — *adj.* **to be beautiful**

(ㅂ) 아름다워
-아름답습니다
-아름다울
-아름다운

한국은 가을에 제일 **아름다워요**.
Korea is the most beautiful in autumn.

저는 **아름다운** 하와이의 바닷가에 가 보고 싶어요.
I'd like to go to the beautiful beaches of Hawaii.

15 **연습(練習)** — *n.* **exercise, practice**
연습하다 [연스파다] — *v.* **to practice**

연습 문제 exercises, exercise questions, 연습실 practice room

현우는 하루에 삼십 분씩 피아노 **연습**을 **했다**.
Hyeonwu practiced playing the piano for thirty minutes every day.

rel. 복습 *n.* **reviewing one's lesson**, 예습 *n.* **previewing one's lesson.**

16 **유행(流行)** *n.* **fashion, trend**
유행하다 *v.* **to be in trend**

이번 여름에는 줄무늬 셔츠가 **유행**이에요.
This summer, striped shirts are in fashion.

요즘 세계에서 K-pop이 **유행하고** 있어요.
Lately, K-pop is becoming a trend worldwide.

17 **자라다** *v.* **to grow (up)**

노아는 시카고에서 태어나서 **자랐어요**.
Noah was born and raised in Chicago.

소피아는 머리가 빨리 **자라서** 미용실에 자주 가요.
Sophia's hair grows quickly, so she goes to the hair salon often.

18 **좋다 [조타]** *adj.* **to be good**

오늘은 날씨가 **좋아요**. The weather is fine today.

저는 **좋은** 친구들이 많아요. I have many good friends.

Note that 좋다 is an adjective and 좋아하다 'to like' is a verb. Thus, the required particles are different in each structure: 나는 사과**가** 좋아요. vs. 나는 사과를 좋아해요. I like apples.

ant. 나쁘다 *adj.* **to be bad** *syn.* 좋아하다 *v.* **to like**
rel. 싫다 *adj.* **to be dislikeable**, 싫어하다 *v.* **to dislike**

19 **착하다 [차카다]** *adj.* **to be nice, good-natured**

내 친구는 정말 **착해요**. 내가 부탁하는 걸 다 해 줘요.
My friend is very nice. He does whatever I ask him to do for me.

20 **표(票)** *n.* **ticket**

비행기 표 airplane ticket, 기차표 train ticket

가: 왜 늦었어요. 영화 곧 시작하겠어요.
Why are you so late? The movie is going to start soon.

나: 미안해요. **표**는 제가 살게요.
I'm sorry. I'll buy the tickets.

CHECK UP

가끔, 날씨, 동네, 모두, 별로, 새로, 시험, 교과서, 소식, 표

1 (not) really, (not) particularly ____________

2 all, all together ____________

3 newly ____________

4 sometimes; once in a while ____________

5 test, exam ____________

6 news ____________

7 village, town; neighborhood area ____________

8 weather ____________

9 textbook ____________

10 ticket ____________

CHECK UP

담그다, 먹다, 바라다, 비싸다, 아름답다, 연습하다,
유행하다, 좋다, 자라다, 착하다

1 to be good-natured ______________________

2 to grow up ______________________

3 to be beautiful ______________________

4 to be expensive ______________________

5 to be good ______________________

6 to eat (food); to drink (liquid); to take (medicine) ______________________

7 to soak, put something in liquid ______________________

8 to wish, want, hope ______________________

9 to practice ______________________

10 to be in trend ______________________

Commonly used Konglish words

1	껌 (gum)	chewing gum
2	노트북 (notebook)	laptop
3	드라이버 (driver)	screw driver
4	러닝머신 (running machine)	treadmill
5	볼펜 (ball pen)	ball point pen
6	리모콘 (remo-con)	remote control
7	샤프 펜슬 (sharp pencil)	mechanical pencil
8	슈퍼 (super)	supermarket
9	스탠드 (stand)	(desk/floor) lamp
10	아르바이트 (arbeit)	part-time job
11	아이스박스 (ice box)	cooler
12	아파트 (apart)	apartment
13	에어컨 (air-con)	air conditioner
14	오토바이 (autobike)	motorcycle
15	원룸 (one room)	studio apartment
16	커닝 (cunning)	cheating (on the exam)
17	파마 (pama)	perm
18	핸드폰 (hand phone)	cellphone
19	핸들 (handle)	steering wheel
20	화이트 (white)	white-out, correction fluid/tape

LESSON

04

1 **가르치다** *v.* to teach; to inform, tell

저희 아버지는 선생님이세요. 고등학교에서 수학을 **가르치세요**.
My father is a teacher. He teaches math at a high school.
우리 형이 저한테 자전거를 **가르쳐** 줬어요.
My brother taught me how to ride a bicycle.

For the meaning 'to inform, tell', this word is always used in 가르쳐 주다/드리다 form. 전화번호 좀 **가르쳐 주세요**. Please tell me your telephone number.

rel. 배우다 to learn → 22-8

2 **교실(教室)** *n.* classroom

한국어 수업에 학생이 많아요. 그래서 한국어 **교실**이 넓어요.
There are many students in my Korean class. So, the Korean classroom is big.

Note that 교실 'classroom' is the physical place for 수업 'class'. A classroom in college is often called 강의실.

3 **낮다** *adj.* to be low

오늘은 어제보다 기온이 더 **낮아요**. 너무 추워요.
Today's temperature is lower than that of yesterday. It is extremely cold.

ant. 높다 *adj.* to be high → 13-3

4 **담배** *n.* cigarette

담배를 피우다 to smoke a cigarette, 담배를 끊다 to quit smoking
여기에서 **담배를 피우지** 마세요. Don't smoke here.

For prohibition of smoking or quitting smoking, 금연 'no smoking' is used as in 금연석 'non-smoking seat'. 이 건물에서는 **금연**이에요. In this building, smoking is prohibited.

5 **동물(動物)** *n.* animal → Appendix B and C

동물원 zoo, 애완동물 pet
저는 **애완동물**을 기르고 싶어요. I would like to raise a pet.

6 **마시다** *v.* **to drink**

저는 커피를 보통 하루에 한 잔 **마셔요**.
I usually drink a cup of coffee every day.

While English verb "to drink" sometimes means "to drink alcoholic beverage," 마시다 alone does not have such a meaning, but you should specify an object as in 물을 마시다 'to drink water', and 술을 마시다 'to drink alcohol'.

7 **모르다** *v.* **to not know, be unaware of, not understand**

(르) 몰라–모릅니다–모를–모르는

저는 저 사람의 이름은 **몰라요**. I don't know the name of that person.
모르는 사람을 따라가면 안 돼요. You should not follow strangers.

ant. 알다 *v.* to know ⋯ 15-14

8 **바람** *n.* **wind; air**

바람이 불다 (wind) to blow
한국은 봄에 **바람**이 세게 **불어요**.
During spring in Korea, the wind blows strongly.

9 **병(病)** *n.* **sickness, illness**

병에 걸리다 to get sick, 병이 낫다 to get well, to be healed, 병원 *n.* hospital
요즘은 날씨가 안 좋아서 **병**에 **걸리는** 사람들이 많아요.
Because the weather has not been good lately, there are many people who are getting sick.
지난 주에 좀 아팠는데 이제는 **병**이 다 **나았어요**.
I was a bit sick last week, but I have recovered now.
제 친구가 어제 **병원**에 입원했어요.
My friend was hospitalized yesterday.

10 **비행기(飛行機)** *n.* **airplane** ⋯ Appendix I

비행기를 타다 to ride an airplane, 비행기 표 airplane ticket
시카고에서 서울까지 **비행기**로 14시간쯤 걸려요.
From Chicago to Seoul, it takes about 14 hours by plane.

A synonym 항공기 'air craft' is used in more official situations or in documents.

11 **색(色)** — *n.* **color**
색깔 — *n.* **color** ⋯→ Appendix M

제일 좋아하는 색이 뭐예요? What is your most favorite color?

이 티셔츠는 색깔이 마음에 안 들어요.
I don't like the color of this T-shirt.

색 and 색깔 are interchangeable in many contexts. However, only 색 can be used as an ending to a color term such as 빨간색 'red', 노란색 'yellow', 파란색 'blue', and 하늘색 'sky blue'.

12 **소포(小包)** — *n.* **package, parcel (as a type of mail)**

친구한테서 소포가 왔어요. I received a package from my friend.

소포 안에 뭐가 들어 있어요? What is in the package?

13 **식다** — *v.* **to cool off, get cold**

국이 아직 뜨거워요. 식기 전에 드세요.
The soup is still hot. Please eat it before it gets cold.

커피가 다 식었네요. My coffee has cooled.

14 **아마** — *adv.* **probably, perhaps**

아마 소피아는 오늘 파티에 못 올 거예요. 내일 시험이 두 개 있어요.
Sophia probably cannot come to the party today. She has two exams tomorrow.

15 **연주(演奏)** — *n.* **musical performance**
연주하다 — *v.* **to play (musical instruments)**

소현이는 고등학교 때 카네기 홀에서 바이올린 연주를 했다.
When Sohyeon was a high school student, she had a violin performance at Carnegie Hall.

16 **은행(銀行)** — *n.* **bank**

은행원 banker

나는 오늘 은행에 가서 돈을 찾고, 슈퍼에 가서 먹을 것을 좀 샀다.
I went to a bank to withdraw money, and purchased something to eat at the supermarket.

rel. 현금 인출기 *n.* **ATM**

17 자전거(自轉車)

n. **bicycle**

세발자전거 tricycle

날씨가 좋은데 공원에 가서 **자전거** 탈래요?

The weather is nice today, so won't you ride a bike at the park?

저는 **자전거**를 타고 학교에 왔어요.

I rode a bicycle and came to school.

18 주다

v. **to give**

현우는 소현이한테 꽃을 **줬어요**.

Hyeonwu gave Sohyeon flowers this morning.

드리다 *v.* to give (humble)

If 주다/드리다 is used after a verb stem in the form of ~어/아 주다/드리다, it means "to do the preceding action for the sake of someone". 저는 남동생에게 음식을 만들어 **줬어요**. I cooked for my younger brother.

지난 달에 할아버지의 70번째 생신이라서 할아버지께 선물을 보내 **드렸습니다**. Last month, I sent a birthday gift to my grandfather who celebrated his 70th birthday.

19 찾다

v. **to look for, find, search; to withdraw money (from the bank or ATM)**

뭐 **찾으세요**? 뭐 잃어버리셨어요?

What are you looking for? Did you lose something?

오늘 아침에 은행에서 10만 원을 **찾았어요**.

This morning, I withdrew 100,000 won from the bank.

syn. 구하다 *v.* **to look for, seek**

20 풀다

(ㄹ) 풀어 – 풉니다 – 풀 – 푸는

v. **to take off (tie, belt, watch); to solve a problem**

인터뷰가 다 끝났어요. 이제 넥타이를 **풀어야겠어요**.

I'm done with the interview. I've got to take off my tie.

스트레스가 있으면 잘 **풀어야** 돼요.

If you have any stress, you should try to relieve it well.

ant. 매다 *v.* **to tie**

CHECK UP

교실, 담배, 동물, 병, 색깔, 아마, 자전거, 비행기, 소포, 은행, 바람

1 animal ....

2 bicycle ....

3 color ....

4 sickness, illness ....

5 airplane ....

6 bank ....

7 cigarette ....

8 classroom ....

9 package, parcel ....

10 probably, perhaps ....

11 wind; air ....

CHECK UP

마시다, 주다, 풀다, 가르치다, 낮다, 모르다, 식다, 연주하다, 찾다

1 to be low ______

2 to cool off ______

3 to look for, find, search; to withdraw money ______

4 to not know, be unaware of, not understand ______

5 to teach, inform, tell ______

6 to drink ______

7 to give ______

8 to take off (tie, belt, watch); to solve a problem ______

9 to perform (musical instruments) ______

Country Names	City Names
한국 Korea	서울 Seoul
타이완/대만 Taiwan	부산 Busan
독일 Germany	베를린 Berlin
몽골/몽고 Mongolia	뉴욕 New York (City)
미국 United States	로스앤젤레스 Los Angeles
베트남 Vietnam	시카고 Chicago
벨기에 Belgium	샌프란시스코 San Francisco
스위스 Switzerland	워싱턴 Washington
영국 England	런던 London
이탈리아/이태리 Italy	파리 Paris
일본 Japan	로마 Rome
중국 China	베이징 Beijing
타이/태국 Thailand	상하이 Shanghai
필리핀 Philippines	도쿄 Tokyo
호주 Australia	시드니 Sydney

LESSON 05

1 **가운데** *n.* **middle (place); center**

한가운데 right in the middle or center

제 책상 **가운데**에 있는 책은 한국어 교과서예요.
The book at the center of my desk is a Korean textbook.

경복궁은 서울 **한가운데**에 있어요.
Gyeongbokgung Palace is right at the center of Seoul.

2 **교통(交通)** *n.* **traffic; transportation**

교통사고 traffic accident, 대중교통 public transportation, 교통 경찰 traffic police Appendix I

서울은 **교통**이 편리해요. 버스나 지하철, 택시를 타고 다닐 수 있어요.
Transportation in Seoul is convenient. You can travel by bus, subway or taxi.

어제 이 길에서 **교통사고**가 났어요.
There was a traffic accident on this road yesterday.

3 **내다** *v.* **to submit, turn in; to pay (money)**

돈을 내다 to pay money

숙제는 금요일에 **내세요**. Submit your homework on Friday.

이 박물관은 **돈을** 안 **내도** 돼요.
You don't have to pay a fee at this museum.

4 **답(答)** *n.* **answer**
답하다 [다파다] *v.* **to answer**

대답하다 *v.* to answer (orally)

이 문제의 **답**을 모르겠어요.
I don't know the answer to this question.

질문에 빨리 **답하세요**. Answer the question quickly.

rel. 질문 *n.* **question** 22-19

5 **동안** *n.* **during, for (time period)**

잠깐 동안 for a short time, 오랫동안 for a long time, 그동안 meanwhile, in the meantime

저는 한국어를 1년 **동안** 공부했어요.
I have studied Korean for 1 year.

그동안 어떻게 지내셨어요? How have you been during this time?

For duration of time, you should not use –에; thus '1년에 공부했어요.' is not grammatical. However, it is possible to omit 동안 as in 저는 한국어를 1년 (동안) 공부했어요.

6 **마음** *n.* **heart, (one's) nature**

마음에 들다 to be in one's like

소현이는 참 **마음이** 따뜻한 친구예요.

Sohyeon is a very warm-hearted friend.

저는 저 빨간색 셔츠가 **마음에 들어요**. I like that red shirt.

While 좋아하다 'to like' describes psychological state of liking something or someone for a certain period of time, 마음에 들다, whose literal meaning is 'to enter one's mind' is used when someone just saw something or someone for the first time and came to like it.

7 **모시다** *v.* **to take (escort) someone (older)**

손님, 어디로 **모실까요**? Customer, where shall I take you?

저는 부모님을 **모시고** 여행을 가려고 해요.

I am intending to take my parents on a trip.

제가 차로 집까지 **모셔다** 드릴게요. I will drive you to your home.

It is often used in such phrases as모시고 가다/오다 'to take and go/come' and 모셔다 드리다 'to take someone to somewhere'. This is used when the subject is in a socially lower position than the object. The plain form of this is 데리다 as used in 데리고 가다/오다 'to take someone (and go/come), or 데려다주다 to take someone

현우는 소현이를 집에 **데려다줬어요**. Hyeonwu took Sohyeon home.

8 **바로** *adv.* **right (there), directly**

여기서 학교까지 **바로** 가는 버스가 있어요?

Is there a bus that goes directly to the school?

은행은 우체국 **바로** 옆에 있어요.

The bank is right next to the post office.

9 **보내다** *v.* **to send (mail, text or money); to spend (time)**

조금 전에 친구들한테 문자를 **보냈어요**.

I just sent a text message to my friends.

주말 잘 **보내세요**. Have a nice weekend.

rel. 지내다 *v.* **to spend (one's) time; to get along** → 16-18

10 빌리다 — *v.* to borrow
빌려주다 — *v.* to lend, rent

저는 친구한테 100달러를 **빌렸어요**.
I borrowed $100 from my friend.
미안하지만 펜 좀 **빌려주세요**.
I'm sorry, but can you lend me a pen?

ant. 갚다 *v.* to pay back

11 생각 — *n.* thought, thinking, idea
생각하다 [생가카다] — *v.* to think

그거 좋은 **생각**이네요. That is a good idea.
저는 돈보다 건강이 중요하다고 **생각해요**.
I think that health is more important than money.

12 소풍 — *n.* picnic, excursion

소풍(을) 가다 to go on a picnic.
날씨가 정말 좋아요. 우리 공원에 **소풍 갈까요**?
The weather is wonderful. Do you want to go for a picnic in the park?

Note that "소풍에 가다" is not a grammatical phrase.

13 식당(食堂) [식땅] — *n.* restaurant, dining hall

이 근처에 한국 **식당**이 있어요?
Is there a Korean restaurant around here?
기숙사 **식당**에서 밥을 먹었어요.
I had meals at the dormitory dining hall.

syn. 음식점 *n.* restaurant → 6-16

14 아이 — *n.* child

디즈니랜드에는 언제나 **아이**들이 많다.
In Disneyland, there are always many children.

'아이' is usually contracted as '애' in colloquial speech. It is also contracted as '얘' from 이 아이 'this kid', 걔 from 그 아이, and 쟤 from 저 아이.

syn. 어린이 *n.* child *ant.* 어른 *n.* adult ···20-14

15 **열(熱)** *n.* **fever, heat**

열이 나다 to run a fever, 열이 내리다 a fever breaks

어제부터 열이 나고 기침이 나요.
I have had a fever and a cough since yesterday.

16 **음료수(飮料水) [음뇨수]** *n.* **beverage**

한국인이 가장 좋아하는 음료수는 커피래요. They say that the most favored beverage of Korean people is coffee.

음료수는 뭐로 하시겠습니까? What would you like to drink?

17 **자주** *adv.* **frequently, often**

저는 도서관에 자주 가요. I go to the library often.

부모님께 자주 전화하세요? Do you often call your parents?

rel. 가끔 *adv.* from time to time, occasionally ···3-1

18 **주로(主–)** *adv.* **mainly, mostly, usually**

저는 주로 도서관에서 공부해요. I study mainly in the library.

rel. 보통 usually, normally ···6-9, 항상 all the time

19 **처음** *n.* **the beginning, the first time**

처음으로 for the first time

안녕하세요? 처음 뵙겠습니다.
Hello. Nice to meet you. (*lit.* It's my first time seeing you.)

이번 여름에 노아는 태어나서 처음으로 한국에 갈 거예요. This summer, Noah is going to go to Korea for the first time in his life.

ant. 마지막 *n.* last ···7-6

20 **피곤하다(疲困–)** *adj.* **to be tired, exhausted**

비행기를 오래 타고 와서 좀 피곤하네요.
Because I had a long flight, I feel a little tired.

오늘은 피곤한 하루였습니다. It was a very tiring day today.

CHECK UP

가운데, 동안, 식당, 열, 교통, 답, 마음, 소풍, 아이, 음료수

1 fever, heat ______

2 during, for (time period) ______

3 traffic; transportation ______

4 answer ______

5 picnic, excursion ______

6 restaurant ______

7 middle (place); center ______

8 child ______

9 beverage ______

10 heart, nature ______

CHECK UP

바로, 빌리다, 주로, 피곤하다, 모시다, 보내다, 생각하다, 자주, 처음, 내다

1 to take (escort) someone (older) ______________________

2 to submit, turn in; to pay (money) ______________________

3 to send (mail or money); to spend (time) ______________________

4 right (there), directly ______________________

5 to borrow ______________________

6 to think ______________________

7 frequently, often ______________________

8 for the first time ______________________

9 mainly, mostly, usually ______________________

10 to be tired, exhausted ______________________

REVIEW Exercises

Choose the one which is most appropriate in the blank.

1 저는 취미로 매일 사진을 ________.

① 그려요 ② 해요 ③ 찍어요 ④ 가져요

2 저는 엄마를 많이 ________.

① 닮았어요 ② 닮아요 ③ 똑같아요 ④ 똑같았어요

3 저는 매주 일요일에 친구들하고 축구를 ________.

① 해요 ② 놀아요 ③ 쳐요 ④ 차요

4 저는 열이 ________ 배가 아파요.

① 식고 ② 내고 ③ 덥고 ④ 나고

5 집에서 학교까지 걸어서 30분쯤 ________.

① 멀어요 ② 걸어요 ③ 걸려요 ④ 다녀요

6 저는 요즘 별로 ________.

① 바빠요 ② 안 바빠요 ③ 잘 지내요 ④ 좋아요

7 저는 한국 음식을 ________.

① 좋아요 ② 좋아해요 ③ 맛있어요 ④ 비싸요

8 한국은 봄에 바람이 세게 ________.

① 불러요 ② 날아요 ③ 나요 ④ 불어요

9 지난 주에는 좀 아팠는데 이제는 병이 다 ________ 내일은 학교에 갈 거예요.

① 걸려서 ② 나아서 ③ 있어서 ④ 없어서

10 이 박물관에 들어갈 때에는 돈을 안 ________ 돼요.

① 벌어도 ② 내도 ③ 받아도 ④ 주면

11 저는 한국어를 1년 ________ 공부했어요.

① 이 ② 에 ③ 밖에 ④ 동안

12 저는 빨간색 셔츠가 마음에 ________.

① 좋아해요 ② 좋아요 ③ 들어요 ④ 괜찮아요

13 여기서는 담배를 ________ 마세요.

① 피지 ② 피우지 ③ 금연하지 ④ 내지

14 저는 어제 시험을 두 개 ________.

① 봤어요 ② 들었어요 ③ 다녔어요 ④ 썼어요

15 한국어 수업에 학생이 많아요. 그래서 한국어 ________이/가 넓어요.

① 수업 ② 반 ③ 교실 ④ 강의

Choose the one that can replace the underlined part.

16 몇 시에 밥을 먹을 거예요?

① 요리를 할 ② 식사를 먹을 ③ 간식을 먹을 ④ 식사를 할

17 저는 한국 식당에서 불고기를 시켰어요.

① 먹었어요 ② 주문했어요 ③ 샀어요 ④ 요리했어요

18 기사 아저씨, 자동차를 너무 빨리 운전하지 마세요.

① 달리지 ② 뛰지 ③ 멈추지 ④ 출발하지

REVIEW Exercises

19 저는 엄마한테 김치 만드는 법을 배웠어요.

① 요리하는 ② 담그는 ③ 놓는 ④ 담는

20 이 신발은 아주 가볍고 편해요.

① 편리해요 ② 피곤해요 ③ 착해요 ④ 편안해요

Choose the one that has the opposite meaning to the underlined part.

21 집이 학교에서 가까워요.

① 멀어요 ② 걸려요 ③ 걸어요 ④ 길어요

22 오늘은 어제보다 기온이 더 낮아요.

① 올라가요 ② 추워요 ③ 짧아요 ④ 높아요

23 오늘 인터뷰가 있어서 넥타이를 매고 왔어요.

① 벗고 ② 차고 ③ 풀고 ④ 입고

24 저는 가끔 운동을 해요.

① 이따가 ② 자주 ③ 또 ④ 아마

25 현우는 아까 기숙사에 갔어요.

① 이따가 ② 방금 ③ 전에 ④ 바로

Answer

1 ③ 2 ① 3 ① 4 ④ 5 ③ 6 ② 7 ② 8 ④ 9 ② 10 ② 11 ④ 12 ③ 13 ② 14 ①
15 ③ 16 ④ 17 ② 18 ① 19 ② 20 ④ 21 ① 22 ④ 23 ③ 24 ② 25 ①

LESSON 06

1 **가족(家族)** *n.* **family**

가족 관계 family relations

가족이 모두 몇 명이에요? How many people are in your family?

가족 generally emphasizes blood relationship, while 식구 refers to family members living in the same house. However, they are often used interchangeably.

2 **구경**
구경하다 *n.* **looking around (with interest); sightseeing**
v. **to look around with interest; to sightsee**

저는 길에서 사람 **구경**하는 것이 재미있어요.
I enjoy watching people on the street.

저는 옷 가게에서 옷을 **구경했어요**.
I looked around in the clothing store.

서울을 다 **구경하려면** 일주일로는 모자라요.
One week is not enough to look around Seoul.

3 **내리다** *v.* **to get off (from transportation); to lower, go down**

어느 지하철 역에서 **내려야** 해요?
At which subway station do I have to get off?

열이 좀 **내렸어요**. The fever has dropped.

오늘은 하루 종일 비가 **내리네요**. It has been raining all day.

ant. 타다 *v.* **to get on (transportation)** ⋯ 19-19
rel. 오르다 *v.* **to go up** ⋯ 13-15

4 **답장(答狀) [답짱]** *n.* **reply letter**

답장을 기다리겠습니다. I will wait for your reply.

지난 주에 부모님께 편지를 보냈는데 오늘 **답장**이 왔어요.
I sent my parents a letter last week, and I got a reply today.

rel. 편지 *n.* **letter** ⋯ 25-19, 이메일 *n.* **email**.

5 **두껍다** *adj.* **to be thick**

(ㅂ) 두꺼워–
–두껍습니다
–두꺼울
–두꺼운

요즘 날씨가 추워서 **두꺼운** 코트를 하나 사려고 해요.
It is cold these days, so I intend to buy a thick coat.

이 책은 너무 **두꺼워서** 다 읽는 데 오래 걸렸어요.
This book is too thick, so it took a long time to read it all.

ant. 얇다 *adj.* to be thin

6 **마중** — *n.* welcoming a person, reception

마중 나가다/나오다 to go/come out to meet (fetch) someone who is coming

가: 공항에 몇 시에 도착하세요? 제가 **마중 나갈게요.**
What time do you arrive at the airport? I will come out to meet you.

나: **마중 나오지** 마세요. 제가 버스 타고 갈게요.
Please don't come out to greet me. I will go by bus.

ant. 배웅 *n.* seeing somebody off

7 **모양** — *n.* shape, form

머리 모양 hair style

이 호수에는 여러 가지 **모양**의 물고기들이 살고 있어요.
There are fishes of various shapes living in this lake.

저 별 **모양** 쿠키는 정말 맛있네요.
That star shape cookie is very delicious.

8 **바르다** — *v.* to apply, spread

(르) 발라요–바릅니다–바를–바른

손가락을 베었어요? 그럼 이 연고를 하루에 세 번 **바르세요.**
Did you cut your finger? Then apply this ointment to the cut three times a day.

빵에 버터를 너무 많이 **발랐어요.**
I spread too much butter on the bread.

9 **보통** — *n./adv.* average; usually, commonly

노아는 키가 **보통**이에요. Noah is of average height.

저는 **보통** 아침 9시에 집에서 나와요.
I normally leave my house at 9:00 am in the morning.

10 **빠르다** — *adj.* to be fast

(르) 빨라–빠릅니다–빠를–빠른

빨리 *adv.* quickly

제 새 컴퓨터는 아주 **빨라요.** My new computer is very fast.

저는 **빠른** 노래를 좋아해요. I like upbeat songs.

ant. 느리다 *adj.* to be slow, *rel.* 천천히 *adv.* slowly

11 생기다 *v.* **to get, obtain something; to happen; to appear, look**

소피아는 요즘 남자 친구가 **생겼어요**. Sophia got a boyfriend recently.

오늘은 좋은 일이 **생길** 것 같아요.
I think good things will happen today.

이 나무는 이상하게 **생겼네요**. This tree looks weird.

잘생기다 'to be handsome' →8-17 and 못생기다 'to be ugly' are derived from the third meaning 'to appear, look'. Note that this form should be used in resultative form 생겼다 to describe the current state.

12 손님 *n.* **guest, customer**

죄송하지만 저는 못 가겠어요. 오늘 집에 **손님**이 와요.
I'm sorry but I can't go with you. I have a guest at home today.

오늘은 가게에 **손님**이 별로 없네요.
There are not very many customers in the store today.

In the commercial settings, for example, in the department store, bank or credit card company, they may use a Sino-Korean word 고객님 'customer' instead of 손님.

무엇을 도와드릴까요, **고객님**? How can I help you, customer?

13 식사(食事) [식싸] *n.* **meal; having a meal**
식사하다 *v.* **to have a meal**

식사하셨어요?
(often used as a greeting) Have you eaten (a meal)?

밥 originally means 'cooked rice', but often refers to 'meal' as in 밥을 먹다 'to eat a meal'. Note that 식사를 먹다 is a wrong phrase.

14 아주 *adv.* **very (much), so, really; extremely; completely**

한국은 여름에 **아주** 덥고 비도 **아주** 많이 온다.
In Korean summer, it is very hot and rains a lot.

내 컴퓨터가 이상했는데, 이제 **아주** 고장났다.
My computer was acting weird, and now it is completely broken.

syn. 정말 →21-17, 참, 매우 →18-6 *adv.* **really, very**

15 열다 — *v.* to open

(ㄹ) 열어 – 엽니다
– 열 – 여는

열리다 *v.* to (be) open

이 식당은 아침 일찍 문을 **열고** 밤 늦게 문을 닫습니다.

This restaurant opens early in the morning and closes late at night.

좀 도와주세요. 문이 잘 안 **열려요**.

Please help me. This door does not open easily.

ant. 닫다 to close 23-3

16 음식(飮食) — *n.* food

음식점 restaurant, 음식을 만들다 to prepare food, to cook

오늘 저녁으로 먹을 **음식**이 없어요.

Today, there is nothing to eat for dinner.

저희 아버지는 지금 **음식**을 **만들고** 계세요.

My father is cooking right now.

syn. 식당 *n.* restaurant 5-13

17 작다 — *adj.* to be small

키가 작다 (height) to be short

나는 손은 **작은데** 발이 크다.

My hands are small, but my feet are big.

제 남동생은 **키가 작아요**. My younger brother is short.

While 작다 is used to describe size, 적다 'to be little' is used for amount.

ant. 크다 *adj.* to be big 17-19

18 주말(週末) — *n.* weekend

벌써 금요일인데, 이번 **주말**에는 뭐 할 거예요?

It's already Friday, so what are you going to do this weekend?

rel. 평일 *n.* weekday 2-20

19 청소(淸掃)
청소하다

n. **cleaning-up**
v. **to clean up**

(진공) 청소기 vacuum cleaner

나는 설거지를 할게. 너는 방 **청소**를 해.
I will wash dishes. You clean up your room.

제 방이 너무 더러워서 **청소해야** 돼요.
Because my room is too dirty, I have to clean it up.

rel. 정리하다 *v.* **to organize**, 닦다 *v.* **to clean, polish**

20 필요하다(必要–)
[피료하다]

adj. **to be needed, necessary**

아직 다 못 했어요. 시간이 좀 더 **필요해요**.
I am not finished yet. I need a little more time.

필요하다 is often translated as 'to need', which is a verb, however 필요하다 is an adjective. So it cannot take any object. Therefore, 저는 돈을 **필요해요**. is grammatically incorrect, but you should say 저는 돈이 **필요해요**. 'I need money' (*lit.* As for me, money is necessary.')

ant. 필요없다 *adj.* **to be not necessary**

CHECK UP

가족, 모양, 보통, 아주, 청소, 답장, 마중, 손님, 음식, 주말

1 average; usually, commonly ....

2 cleaning-up ....

3 family ....

4 shape, form ....

5 food ....

6 guest, customer ....

7 welcoming a person, reception ....

8 reply letter ....

9 extremely; completely ....

10 weekend ....

CHECK UP

구경하다, 바르다, 빠르다, 필요하다, 내리다, 두껍다,
생기다, 식사하다, 열다, 작다

1 to be small ....

2 to be thick ....

3 to get off (from transportation); to lower, go down ....

4 to get, obtain something; to happen; to appear, look ....

5 to have a meal ....

6 to open ....

7 to apply, spread ....

8 to be fast ....

9 to be needed, necessary ....

10 to sightsee ....

LESSON

07

1 **간식(間食)** *n.* **snack; food eaten between meals**

간식 시간 snack time

소현이는 살찌는 게 싫어서 **간식**을 안 먹어요.
Sohyeon doesn't want to gain weight so she doesn't eat snacks.

2 **구름** *n.* **cloud**

구름이 끼다 to get cloudy

오늘은 **구름**이 많이 **끼었네요**. There are lots of clouds today.

공연에 사람들이 **구름**처럼 모여들었어요.
People gathered at the concert like clouds.

rel. 흐리다 to be cloudy ⋯23-20

3 **너무** *adv.* **too much; very**

이번 학기는 수업이 많아서 **너무** 바빠요.
I have a lot of classes this semester, so I'm very busy.

옷이 **너무** 커서 입을 수가 없어요.
These clothes are so big that I can't possibly wear them.

너무 originally has somewhat negative connotation for describing excessive state, but these days, it is often used without such a connotation. Sometimes, 너무 is repeated to emphasize. 소현이의 여동생은 **너무너무** 귀여워요. Sohyeon's younger sister is very very cute.

4 **대단히** *adv.* **very much; extremely**
대단하다 *adj.* **to be huge, enormous, great**

항상 도와주셔서 **대단히** 감사합니다.
Thank you so much for helping me all the time.

한국어 말하기 실력이 **대단하시네요**!
Your Korean speaking ability is great!

syn. 굉장히 *adv.* very much ⋯2-2

5 **두다** *v.* **to put, place, leave**

책을 책상 위에 **두세요**. Please put the book on the desk.

과일은 냉장고에 넣어 **두세요**.
Keep your food in the refrigerator.

6 **마지막** — *n.* **the last**

마지막으로 finally, lastly

내가 너를 도와주는 것은 이번이 **마지막**이야.
This is the last time I will help you.

마지막 열차는 밤 12시 30분에 와요. The last train comes at 12:30 am.

제가 **마지막으로** 하고 싶은 말은 저는 죄가 없다는 것입니다.
The last thing I want to say is that I am innocent.

ant. 처음 *n.* **the beginning** 5-19

7 **모으다** — *v.* **to gather; to collect, accumulate**

(ㅡ) 모아–모읍니다–모을–모으는

돈을 모으다 to save money

저는 취미로 외국 인형들을 **모아요**. As a hobby, I collect foreign dolls.

저는 아르바이트를 해서 **모은** 돈으로 여행 갈 거예요.
With the money saved from part-time jobs, I will go on a trip.

8 **바쁘다** — *adj.* **to be busy**

(ㅡ) 바빠–바쁩니다–바쁠–바쁜

요즘 숙제도 많고 시험도 있어서 너무 **바빠요**.
I am extremely busy these days because I have too much homework and too many exams.

바쁘다 should take an animate subject (person or animal). For the following expressions with "busy", you should not use 바쁘다.
The line is busy. 통화 중이에요.
The street is busy today. 오늘은 길이 복잡해요.

ant. 한가하다 *adj.* **to be free**

9 **복도(複道) [복또]** — *n.* **hallway**

화장실은 이 **복도** 끝 오른쪽에 있어요.
The restroom is on the right at the end of this hallway.

10 **빨다** — *v.* **to wash clothes**

(ㄹ) 빨아–빱니다–빨–빠는

빨래 laundry, 빨래하다 to do the laundry, 빨래방 laundromat

이 옷은 더러워서 **빨아야** 돼요.
I have to wash these clothes because they are dirty.

저는 일주일에 한 번 **빨래**를 해요. I do the laundry once a week.

rel. 세탁기 *n.* **washing machine** 24-10

11 생일(生日) *n.* **birthday**

생일이 언제예요? When is your birthday?

생일 축하합니다! Happy birthday!

생신 *n.* birthday (honorific form)

할아버지, 생신 축하드립니다! Grandpa, happy birthday!

One's first birthday is specially called 돌 or 첫돌 ···› 24-4

12 손수건 [손쑤건] *n.* **handkerchief**

울지 마세요. 여기 제 손수건을 쓰세요.
Please do not cry. Here, use my handkerchief.

13 식탁(食卓) *n.* **dining table**

식탁을 차리다 to set the table

배고프지? 이리 와서 식탁에 앉아.
You are hungry, aren't you? Come here and have a seat at the table.

Korean style dining table for sitting around on the floor is called 밥상. ···› Appendix D

14 아직 *adv.* **still, yet**

내일 시험인데 시험 공부를 아직 다 못 했어.
I have an exam tomorrow, but I have not finished studying for it yet.

아직 is usually used in sentences with negation expressions. It usually compares with 벌써 'already', which usually goes with affirmative sentences. ···› 25-8

저는 **아직** 다 **안** 했어요. I didn't finish it yet.

나는 벌써 다 했어. I have already finished it.

15 열심히 [열씸히] *adv.* **hard, diligently**

좋은 성적을 위해서 열심히 공부했어요.
For a better grade, I studied hard.

우리 아버지는 가족을 위해서 열심히 일하세요.
My father works hard for our family.

16 **음악(音樂)** *n.* **music**

음악가 musician, 음악을 듣다 to listen to music, 음악회 musical concert

저는 클래식 **음악**을 별로 좋아하지 않아요.
I don't like classical music that much.

저는 매일 한국 **음악**을 **들어요**. I listen to Korean music every day.

17 **잘못** *n.* **wrong; anything done wrong**
잘못하다[잘모타다] *v.* **to make a mistake**

학교 오는 버스를 **잘못** 타서 수업 시간에 늦었다.
I was late to the class because I took the wrong bus to school.

교통사고가 났어. 내 **잘못**은 아니야.
I had a car accident. It's not my fault.

제가 **잘못했어요**. 죄송해요.
It's my fault. Sorry.

18 **주문하다(注文-)** *v.* **to order**

인터넷에서 물건을 **주문하면**, 집에 오는 데 이틀밖에 안 걸려요.
If I order something online, it takes just two days to be delivered to my house.

rel. 시키다 **to order (food)** → 2-13

19 **축하하다(祝賀-) [추카하다]** *v.* **to congratulate**

현우야, 생일 **축하해**. Hyeonwu, happy birthday to you.

졸업을 **축하합니다**. Congratulations on your graduation.

축하해 주셔서 감사합니다. Thank you for congratulating me.

20 **하늘** *n.* **sky**

하늘색 sky blue

한국은 가을에 **하늘**이 더 높고 파래요.
In Korea, the sky looks higher and bluer in fall.

CHECK UP

간식, 구름, 너무, 복도, 생일, 식탁, 열심히, 손수건, 음악, 하늘

1 birthday ______________________

2 dining table ______________________

3 hallway ______________________

4 hard, diligently ______________________

5 snack; food eaten between meals ______________________

6 cloud ______________________

7 handkerchief ______________________

8 music ______________________

9 too much; very ______________________

10 sky ______________________

CHECK UP

대단히, 마지막, 바쁘다, 빨다, 아직, 잘못하다, 주문하다,
모으다, 축하하다, 두다

1 to congratulate ....

2 to gather; to collect, accumulate ....

3 to put, place ....

4 still, yet ....

5 the last ....

6 to be busy ....

7 to make a mistake, do something wrong ....

8 to order ....

9 to wash clothes ....

10 very much; extremely ....

Question Words

Choose the word that best fills in the blank. You may use the same word multiple times.

뭐(=무엇), 무슨, 어느, 얼마나, 얼마, 어디, 언제, 왜, 어떻게, 누구, 몇

1 가: ________ 한국어 수업이 끝났어요?
나: 30분 전에 끝났어요.

2 가: 오늘이 ________ 요일이에요?
나: 오늘은 수요일이에요.

3 가: 그동안________ 지냈어요?
나: 좀 바빴어요.

4 가: ________ 나라 사람이에요?
나: 저는 미국 사람이에요.

5 가: ________하고 영화를 봤어요?
나: 제 동생하고 영화를 봤어요.

6 가: 올해 ________살이에요?
나: 스무 살이에요.

7 가: 화장실이 ________에 있어요?
나: 복도 끝에서 왼쪽으로 가세요.

8 가: 지금 ________시예요?
나: 3시 15분이요.

9 가: 집에서 학교까지 ________ 걸려요?
나: 걸어서 10분 걸려요.

10 가: 이거 ________예요?
나: 15000원이에요.

11 가: ________오셨어요?
나: 저, 김민수 교수님을 만나러 왔는데요.

12 가: 어제 학교에 ________ 안 왔어요?
나: 감기에 걸려서 병원에 갔어요.

Answer

1 언제 **2** 무슨 **3** 어떻게 **4** 어느 **5** 누구 **6** 몇 **7** 어디 **8** 몇 **9** 얼마나 **10** 얼마 **11** 어떻게 **12** 왜

LESSON 08

1 **감기** — *n.* **cold**

코감기 sinus cold, 목감기 sore throat

감기에 걸리다 to catch a cold

저는 감기에 걸렸어요. I have a cold.

"저는 **감기**에 걸렸어요." literally means "I have been caught by a cold."; so note that you have to use the resultative form 걸렸어요 to mean "I have a cold."

2 **귀엽다** — *adj.* **to be cute**

(ㅂ) 귀여워–귀엽습니다–귀여울–귀여운

귀여워하다 *v.* to love (on), adore

소현이는 웃을 때 귀여워요. Sohyeon is cute when she smiles.

저는 귀여운 남자를 좋아해요. I like cute boys.

우리 누나는 개를 귀여워해요. My older sister adores our dog.

3 **넓다 [널따]** — *adj.* **to be wide; to be spacious**

한국어 교실이 아주 넓어요. My Korean classroom is very large.

이 길이 아주 넓어요. This street is very wide.

ant. 좁다 *adj.* **to be narrow** → 25-17

4 **대답하다(對答–) [대다파다]** — *v.* **to answer, give a reply**

대답 — *n.* **answer, response**

제 질문에 대답해 주세요. Please answer my question.
왜 대답이 없어요? Why don't you answer me?

ant. 물어보다 *v.* **to ask**

5 **드리다** — *v.* **to give (humble)**

저는 아버지께 선물을 드렸어요. I gave my father a gift.

도와 드리다 to help (a respectable person)

저는 아버지를 **도와 드렸어요**. I helped my father.

드리다 is used when the recipient is a socially higher person than the giver. When a socially higher person gives something to a socially lower person, 주시다, honorific form of 주다, should be used: 아버지는 저한테 선물을 **주셨어요**. Father gave me a gift.

6 마치다 — *v.* **to finish, complete**

마침표 period mark

김 교수님은 오후 3시에 수업을 **마치세요**. Professor Kim will finish the class at 3:00 pm.

syn. 끝내다 *v.* to finish, *ant.* 시작하다 *v.* to start ⋯→ 24-11

7 모이다 — *v.* **to get together**

모임 *n.* gathering, meeting

어제 동창 모임에 많은 친구들이 **모였어요**.
Many friends gathered at the alumni gathering yesterday.

모이다 is a passive form of 모으다 'to collect' ⋯→ 7-7.

8 박물관(博物館) [방물관] — *n.* **museum**

국립 중앙 **박물관**은 서울 용산에 있어요.
The National Museum of Korea is in Yongsan, Seoul.

rel. 미술관 *n.* art museum

9 복잡하다(複雜–) [복짜파다] — *adj.* **to be crowded; to be complicated**

서울은 아주 **복잡한** 도시예요.
Seoul is a crowded city.

이 수학 문제는 너무 **복잡해요**.
This math problem is too complicated.

10 빼다 — *v.* **to take off (accessories or gloves); to pull out; to subtract**

저는 집에 가면 바로 반지와 귀걸이를 **빼요**.
I take off my rings and earrings when I go back home.

비빔밥에서 고추장은 **빼** 주세요.
Please take spicy pepper sauce out of bibimbap.

ant. 끼다 *v.* to put on (rings, gloves)

11 생활(生活) *n.* **life, living**

생활비 the cost of living

요즘 학교 **생활**이 어떠세요?

How has your school life been recently?

서울에서는 **생활비**가 많이 들지요?

The cost of living in Seoul is expensive, right?

12 수고하다 *n.* **to make an effort, to take the trouble**

일 다 끝나셨어요? **수고하셨어요**.

Is all your work done now? Thank you (for the work).

선생님, 수업 하시느라 **수고하셨습니다**.

Teacher, thank you for your effort for the classes.

13 신기하다 (神奇-/新奇-) *adj.* **to be amazing, wonderful; novel, new**

젓가락으로 어떻게 콩을 집어요? 정말 **신기해요**.

How can you pick up beans with chopsticks? It's so amazing.

14 아프다 *adj.* **to be sick; painful**

(—) 아파 – 아픕니다 – 아플 – 아픈

선생님, 제가 어제 머리가 너무 **아파서** 숙제를 못 했어요.

Teacher, I couldn't do the homework because I had a terrible headache yesterday.

넘어져서 무릎을 다쳤습니다. 무릎이 너무 **아픕니다**.

I hurt my knees falling on the ground. My knees really hurt.

15 영화(映畫) *n.* **movie**

영화관 movie theater, 영화배우 movie actor/actress, 영화 표 movie ticket, 영화를 보다 to watch a movie

이번 주말에 저하고 같이 **영화** 보러 갈래요?

Will you go to the movies with me this weekend?

rel. 극장 *n.* **theater** → 11-2

16 이기다

v. to win, beat

어제 라이벌 팀을 **이겨서** 정말 기뻤다.
I was so happy because we won against the rival team.

Korean 이기다 is used as in 시합을/시합에서 이기다 'to win the game' or 'to beat the opposing team', but different verbs are used for other phrases such as 상을 타다/받다 'to win the prize', or 100달러를 따다 'to win $100 (at the gamble)'.

ant. 지다 *v.* to lose ⋯ 17-18

17 잘생기다

adj. to be handsome

소피아의 아빠는 배우처럼 정말 **잘생기셨다**.
Sophia's dad is really handsome like an actor.

To describe that somebody is handsome, you have to use it in the resultative (past) form as 잘생겼다.

ant. 못생기다 *adj.* to be ugly

18 주소(住所)

n. address

이메일 주소 email address, 홈페이지 주소 homepage address

가: 거기에 어떻게 가실 거예요?
How can you get there?

나: **주소**만 알려 주시면 제가 찾아갈게요.
I'll go there if you just tell me the address.

19 춤

n. dance

(춤을) 추다 to dance

저는 음악은 좋아하는데 **춤**은 안 좋아해요.
I like music but not dancing.

TV에서 제가 좋아하는 가수가 **춤**을 **추면**서 노래를 부르고 있어요.
My favorite singer is singing and dancing on TV.

20 학기(學期) [학끼]

n. semester, academic term

이번 **학기**에는 수업을 많이 들어서 바빠요.
I'm busy taking many courses this semester.

저는 이번 방학에 여름 **학기** 수업을 들을 거예요.
I am going to take summer session classes during this vacation.

CHECK UP

감기, 생활, 수고, 영화, 춤, 모임, 박물관, 주소, 학기, 대답

1 cold ....

2 dance ....

3 life, living ....

4 movie ....

5 address ....

6 museum ....

7 semester, academic term ....

8 answer, reply ....

9 making an effort, taking the trouble ....

10 gathering ....

CHECK UP

귀엽다, 신기하다, 마치다, 빼다, 아프다, 이기다, 넓다, 드리다, 복잡하다, 잘생기다

1 to be amazing, wonderful; novel, new ....

2 to be crowded; to be complicated ....

3 to be handsome ....

4 to be cute ....

5 to be sick; painful ....

6 to finish, complete ....

7 to take off (accessories or gloves); to pull out; to subtract ....

8 to win, beat ....

9 to be wide; to be spacious ....

10 to give (humble) ....

Error Correction 1

The following sentences have some errors. Please find them and make corrections.

1 마이클은 제 친구가 이에요.

2 민수는 한국에서 3년에 공부했어요.

3 민지는 제 제일 친구예요.

4 수업 시간에는 선생님을 잘 들어야 해요.

5 양말을 꼭 입으세요.

6 영수는 민지를 결혼하고 싶어해요.

7 저는 매일 도서관에 공부해요.

8 저는 매일 커피가 마셨어요.

9 저는 버스를 타서 학교에 와요.

10 저는 부모님을 매일 전화해요.

Answer

1 마이클은 제 친구예요.
2 민수는 한국에서 3년 동안 공부했어요.
3 민제는 제 제일 친한 친구예요.
4 수업 시간에는 선생님 말씀을 잘 들어야 해요.
5 양말을 꼭 신으세요.
6 영수는 민지하고 결혼하고 싶어해요.
7 저는 매일 도서관에서 공부해요.
8 저는 매일 커피를 마셨어요.
9 저는 버스를 타고 학교에 와요.
10 저는 부모님께 매일 전화해요.

LESSON

09

1 **갈다 [갇따]** *adj.* **to be the same**

똑같다 to be exactly the same

저는 소현이하고 고향이 **같아요**.

Sohyeon and I came from the same hometown.

현우는 동생하고 키가 **똑같아요**.

Hyeonwu and his younger brother are the same height.

~(으)ㄴ/는 것 같다 seems like, looks like

오늘은 추운 **것 같아요**. It seems to be cold today.

제 룸메이트는 지금 컴퓨터 게임을 하**는 것 같아요**. It looks like my roommate is playing a computer game.

ant. 다르다 *adj.* **to be different** ···17-3

2 **그동안** *n.* **meanwhile, during the time**

그동안 어떻게 지내셨어요? How have you been during this time?

rel. 동안 *n.* **during, for (time period)** ···5-5

3 **넣다 [너타]** *v.* **to put in**

이 음식이 짜요. 소금을 너무 많이 **넣었어요**.

This dish is salty. You put too much salt in.

여기서 주머니에 손을 **넣고** 걸으면 위험해요.

It is dangerous to walk with your hands in your pockets here.

ant. 꺼내다 *v.* **to take out**

4 **대부분(大部分)** *n.* **most part of something;** *adv.* **mostly**

내 친한 친구들 **대부분**이 장학금을 받아요.

The majority of my close friends receive scholarships.

저는 이 파티에 온 사람들을 **대부분** 알아요.

I know most of the people at this party.

5 **드시다** *v.* **to eat (honorific)** ···3-6

차린 건 없지만 많이 **드세요**.

I didn't prepare a lot, but please help yourself.

오늘 점심에 뭐 **드실래요**?

What do you want to eat for lunch today?

This verb 드시다 and 식사하시다 are commonly used honorific words of 먹다. They are sufficiently polite words, but some senior adults may like (진지) 잡수시다 which sounds even more polite.

6 **막히다 [마키다]** *v.* **to be blocked, congested**

감기에 걸려서 코가 **막혔어요**.
I caught a cold and my nose is congested.
이 길은 매일 **막혀요**. This road is congested every day.

7 **목욕하다 [모교카다]** *v.* **to take a bath**

목욕탕 bathroom, 대중 목욕탕 public bath house
따뜻한 물에 **목욕**을 하면 잘 잘 수 있어요.
If you take a hot bath, you can sleep well.

목욕탕 refers to a place where you can take a bath, so it is not used to refer to public restrooms (화장실).

8 **박수(拍手) [박쑤]** *n.* **handclap, applause**

박수를 치다 to clap one's hand, 박수를 보내다 to give someone a clap
여러분, 이 가수들에게 큰 **박수** 부탁 드립니다.
Everyone, please give the singers here a big round of applause.

syn. 손뼉 *n.* clap

9 **볶다 [복따]** *v.* **to stir fry, roast** → Appendix E

볶음밥 fried rice
프라이팬에 기름을 조금 두르고 양파를 **볶으세요**.
Put some oil on the pan and stir fry the onions.

rel. 튀기다 *v.* to deep-fry

10 **사거리(四–)** *n.* **intersection** → Appendix F

저 **사거리**에서 왼쪽으로 가면 학교가 나와요.
If you turn left at that intersection, you can go to the school.

syn. 네거리 *n.* intersection,
rel. 삼거리 *n.* three-way intersection

11 **서다** *v.* **to stand; to stop, halt**

줄을 서다 to stay in line

버스에 자리가 없어서 집에 오는 동안 계속 **서** 있었어요.
There were no seats available on the bus, so I remained standing until I got home.

기차표를 사려면 여기에서 **줄을 서세요**.
If you want to buy a train ticket, wait in line here.

이 엘리베이터는 5층에서 안 **서요**.
This elevator does not stop at the 5th floor.

rel. 앉다 *v.* **to sit** ⋯ 13-14, 눕다 *v.* **to lie down**

12 **수도(首都)** *n.* **capital city of a country**

한국의 **수도**는 서울이에요. The capital of Korea is Seoul.

rel. 도시 *n.* **city** ⋯ 20-4

13 **신나다** *v.* **to be excited, to be exciting**

이번 주말에는 여행을 가서 아주 **신나요**!
Since I'm going on a trip this weekend, I'm so excited!

저는 **신나는** 음악을 좋아해요. I like lively music.

Note that 신나다 is translated as an adjective in English, but it is a verb as conjugated 신난다 and 신나는.

14 **악기(樂器) [악끼]** *n.* **musical instrument**

악기를 연주하다 to play/perform on instruments

제가 제일 좋아하는 **악기**는 바이올린이에요.
My favorite musical instrument is the violin.

15 **예쁘다** *adj.* **to be pretty, beautiful**

(—) 예뻐 – 예쁩니다 – 예쁠 – 예쁜

노아의 여자 친구는 정말 **예뻐요**.
Noah's girlfriend is really pretty.

In colloquial speech, 이쁘다 is used in many cases, yet it is not a standard form.

rel. 아름답다 *adj.* **to be beautiful** ⋯ 3-4

16 이따가/이따 *adv.* **little later**

지금은 너무 바쁘니까 이따가 다시 전화하세요.
As I am so busy right now, please give me a call a little later.

syn. 나중에 *adv.* later

17 잘하다 *v.* **to do well**

한국어를 잘하시네요. You speak Korean well.
아주 잘했어요. Excellent job!

ant. 못하다 *v.* cannot do
rel. 잘못하다 to make a mistake 7-17

18 주일(週日) *n.* **a week**

이번 주(일) this week, 다음 주(일) next week
소피아는 일주일에 세 번은 조깅을 해요.
Sophia goes jogging three times a week.
이번 주일은 시험이 많아서 바빠요.
I am busy this week because I have many exams.

syn. 주 *n.* a week

19 춥다 *adj.* **to be cold**

(ㅂ) 추워 – 춥습니다 – 추울 – 추운

이번 겨울은 눈도 많이 오고, 날씨도 너무 추워요.
This winter, it snows a lot and it is very cold.

춥다 refers to your feeling cold due to low temperature and such. You should use 차갑다 or 차다 when a certain object (including air) is cold when you touch it.
커피가 차갑다. The coffee is cold.

ant. 덥다 *adj.* to be hot 16-4

20 한자(漢字) [한짜] *n.* **Chinese character**

한자를 많이 알면 한국어를 공부하는 데에 도움이 돼요.
If you know many Chinese characters, it is helpful to study Korean.

CHECK UP

그동안, 대부분, 박수, 사거리, 수도, 악기, 이따가, 주일, 한자

1 capital city of a country ____________

2 Chinese character ____________

3 during the time ____________

4 handclap, applause ____________

5 intersection ____________

6 little later ____________

7 most part of something; mostly ____________

8 musical instrument ____________

9 a week ____________

CHECK UP

같다, 넣다, 드시다, 막히다, 목욕하다, 볶다, 서다, 신나다, 예쁘다, 잘하다, 춥다

1 to be blocked, congested ....

2 to be cold ....

3 to be excited, to be exciting ....

4 to be pretty, beautiful ....

5 to be the same ....

6 to do well ....

7 to eat (honorific form of 먹다) ....

8 to put in ....

9 to stand; to stop, halt ....

10 to stir fry, roast ....

11 to take a bath ....

Error Correction 2

The following sentences have some errors. Please find them and make corrections.

1. 저는 새 옷을 필요해요.
2. 저는 어제 오후에 일에 갔어요.
3. 저는 자동차를 있어요.
4. 저는 친구 같이 점심을 먹었어요.
5. 저는 키가 150cm예요. 저는 짧아요.
6. 저는 한국 친구를 많아요.
7. 저희 부모님은 한국에 있으세요.
8. 제 남자친구는 아주 잘 생겨요.
9. 제 동생은 매일 컴퓨터 게임을 놀아요.
10. 저는 아직 식사를 안 먹었어요.

Answer

1. 저는 새 옷이 필요해요.
2. 저는 오후에 일하러 갔어요.
3. 저는 자동차가 있어요.
4. 저는 친구하고 같이 점심을 먹었어요.
5. 저는 키가 150cm예요. 저는 키가 작아요.
6. 저는 한국 친구가 많아요.
7. 저희 부모님은 한국에 계세요.
8. 제 남자친구는 아주 잘 생겼어요.
9. 제 동생은 매일 컴퓨터 게임을 해요.
10. 저는 아직 식사를 안 했어요.

LESSON 10

1 **같이 [가치]** *adv.* **together**

저는 제 친구하고 **같이** 영화를 봤어요.
I watched a movie (together) with my friend.

Note that "저는 친구 같이 영화를 봤어요." is not a correct sentence to mean 'I watched a movie with a friend.' You need a particle such as 하고, 와/과, or (이)랑 'with' after 친구. Further, it is possible to omit 같이 as follows: 저는 친구하고 (친구랑/친구와) (같이) 영화를 봤어요. I watched a movie with my friend. 같이 may be omitted here.

2 **그리다** *v.* **to draw**
그림 *n.* **painting, drawing**

그림을 그리다 to draw paintings or pictures
현우는 공원에서 **그림을 그리고** 있어요.
Hyeonwu is painting at the park.
소현이는 미술 시간에 장미를 **그렸어요**.
Sohyeon draw roses in the art class.

3 **노래** *n.* **song**

노래(를) 하다, 노래(를) 부르다 to sing a song
노래방 noraebang, *karaoke* (place)
지금 무슨 **노래**를 듣고 있어요?
What song are you listening to now?

4 **대통령(大統領) [대통녕]** *n.* **president of a country**

한국의 **대통령**이 미국을 방문했습니다.
The president of Korea visited the United States.
미국의 첫 번째 **대통령은** 조지 워싱턴이에요.
The first president of the United States was George Washington.

5 **듣다** *v.* **to listen; to take a course**

(ㄷ) 들어요
~~듣습니다~~
~~들을 듣는~~

저는 학교에 오면서 음악을 **들어요**.
I listen to the music on the way to school.
우리가 같이 **들은** 과목이 세 개예요?
Did we take three courses together?

듣다 cannot directly take a person as an object; therefore 선생님을 듣다 is not a grammatically correct phrase. You should say something like 선생님 말씀을 잘 들으세요. 'Listen to your teacher carefully.'

6 **만나다** *v.* **to meet**

만남 meeting

내일 몇 시에 **만날까요**? What time shall we meet tomorrow?

제가 어제 **만난** 사람은 고등학교 때 친구예요.
The person I met yesterday is a friend that I met in high school.

ant. 헤어지다 *v.* **to part, break up**

7 **못하다[모타다]** *v.* **to be unable to do; cannot do**

잘 못하다 cannot do well

저는 노래는 **잘 못해요**. I cannot sing well.

저는 중국어를 **못해요**. I cannot speak Chinese.

~지 못하다 indicates that the subject is unable to do that action. 이곳에서는 사람이 살**지 못해요**. (=이곳에서는 사람이 못 살아요.) People cannot live at this place.

8 **반찬(飯饌)** *n.* **side dish** → Appendix D

한국에서 밥하고 같이 먹는 음식들을 **반찬**이라고 해요.
In Korean cuisine, food eaten along with cooked rice is called *banchan*.

김치는 한국 사람들에게 아주 중요한 **반찬**이에요.
Kimchi is a very important banchan for Korean people.

9 **봉투(封套)** *v.* **envelope; bag (for grocery or garbage)**

편지 봉투 letter envelope, 쓰레기 봉투 garbage bag

한국에서는 쓰레기는 꼭 **쓰레기 봉투**에 넣어서 버려야 해요.
In Korea, you have to throw away garbage in garbage bags.

10 **사고(事故)** *n.* **accident**

교통사고 traffic accident, 사고가 나다 an accident occurs

조심하세요. 이 길에서는 **교통사고**가 잘 **나요**.
Watch out. Many traffic accidents occur on this road.

11 **서로** — *adv.* **each other, one another**

현우와 소현이는 **서로** 좋아해요.
Hyeonwu and Sohyeon like each other.
우리는 모두 **서로** 도와줘야 해요.
We all have to help each other.

12 **수업(授業)** — *n.* **class**

수업을 듣다 to take a class
수업 중에는 선생님 말씀을 잘 들어야 해요.
You must listen to your teacher carefully during class.
한국어 **수업**은 어느 교실에서 해요?
In which classroom does the Korean class meet?

You can count 수업 with the counter 과목 or 개 as in 저는 이번 학기에 수업을 다섯 개 (or 과목) 들어요.

13 **신문(新聞)** — *n.* **newspaper**

신문지 newspaper (refers to the material paper)
가: 뉴스를 어디서 보세요? Where do you check the news?
나: 저는 인터넷 **신문**에서 봐요. I check it on the internet newspaper.

14 **안녕하다(安寧–)** — *adj.* **to be well; feel well**

안녕히 *adv.* well
안녕하세요? How are you? (*lit.* Are you all right?)
고향에 계신 우리 할아버지, 할머니는 모두 **안녕하십니다**.
My grandfather and grandmother in my hometown are doing well.
안녕히 가세요. (to someone leaving) Good bye. (*lit.* Go safely.)

15 **예약(豫約)** — *n.* **reservation, appointment**
예약하다 [예야카다] — *v.* **to make a reservation/appointment**

들어요–듣습니다

병원에 **예약**을 했어요?
Did you make an appointment for the hospital?
다음 주에 여행을 가기 위해 비행기와 호텔을 **예약했다**.
I reserved a flight and a hotel for the trip scheduled next week.

rel. 약속 *n.* **appointment; promise** →17-4

16 **이발소(理髮所) [이발쏘]** *n.* barber shop

남자들은 주로 **이발소**에서 머리를 자른다.
Men usually go to the barbershop to get a haircut.

rel. 미용실/미장원 *n.* beauty salon

17 **잠깐** *n.* short time; *adv.* for a moment, briefly

슈퍼에서 살 게 있어요. **잠깐만** 기다려 주세요. I have to buy something at the supermarket. Please wait here for just a moment.

syn. 잠시 *adv.* for a moment

18 **죽다** *v.* to die

이 년 전에 우리 개가 **죽었어요**. 정말 슬펐어요.
My dog died two years ago. I was really sad.

The honorific form of 죽다 is 돌아가시다. →25-4
저희 할아버지는 10년 전에 **돌아가셨어요**. My grandfather passed away 10 years ago.

ant. 살다 *v.* to live →24-9

19 **취미(趣味)** *n.* hobby; interest

저는 **취미**로 한국 요리를 배우고 싶어요.
As a hobby, I want to learn how to cook Korean food.
가: **취미**가 뭐예요? What is your hobby?
나: 저는 영화 보는 것을 좋아해요. I like watching movies.

20 **해** *n.* the sun

해가 뜨다 The sun rises. 해가 지다 The sun sets.
햇빛 sunlight, sunshine
현우야, 일어나. **해**가 벌써 **떴어**.
Wake up, Hyeonwu! The sun is already up.

해가 서쪽에서 뜨겠다. 'The sun will rise in the West.' is an expression for describing something impossible or very rare in an exaggerated way.
현우가 이렇게 일찍 일어나다니 **해가 서쪽에서 뜨겠어요**. It is a miracle to see Hyeonwu get up so early this morning!

syn. 태양 *n.* the sun; *rel.* 달 *n.* the moon

CHECK UP

노래, 봉투, 사고, 신문, 취미, 반찬, 대통령, 이발소, 수업, 해

1 accident ....

2 barber shop ....

3 class ....

4 envelope; bag (for grocery or garbage) ....

5 hobby; interest ....

6 newspaper ....

7 president of a country ....

8 side dish ....

9 song ....

10 the sun ....

CHECK UP

만나다, 안녕하다, 예약하다, 같이, 죽다, 못하다, 듣다, 그리다, 서로, 잠깐

1 each other, one another ....

2 short time; for a moment, briefly ....

3 to be unable to; cannot do ....

4 to be well; feel well ....

5 to die ....

6 to draw ....

7 to listen to; to take a course ....

8 to make a reservation /appointment ....

9 to meet ....

10 together ....

REVIEW Exercises

Choose the one which is most appropriate in the blank.

1 저는 요즘 남자 친구가 ____________.

① 생겼어요 ② 있어졌어요 ③ 가졌어요 ④ 생겨졌어요

2 안녕하세요? 식사 ________________?

① 드리셨어요 ② 먹었어요 ③ 먹으셨어요 ④ 하셨어요

3 차린 건 없지만 많이 ____________.

① 드세요 ② 먹으세요 ③ 식사드세요 ④ 맛있어요

4 아버지께서 저한테 선물을 __________.

① 드렸어요 ② 주셨어요 ③ 줬어요 ④ 드리셨어요

5 저는 아버지께 선물을 __________.

① 줬어요 ② 주셨어요 ③ 드렸어요 ④ 드리셨어요

6 저는 이번 학기에 수업을 네 과목 ____________.

① 봐요 ② 들어요 ③ 다녀요 ④ 가요

7 이 영화의 남자 배우는 정말 ______________.

① 잘생겨요 ② 잘생겼어요 ③ 어울려요 ④ 잘 예뻐요

8 주말에는 많은 사람들이 춤을 ____________ 클럽에 가요.

① 하러 ② 부르러 ③ 놀러 ④ 추러

9 음식에 소금을 조금만 ______________.

① 놓으세요 ② 넣으세요 ③ 담그세요 ④ 드세요

10 길에 자동차가 많아서 교통이 ________________.

① 바빠요 ② 복잡해요 ③ 막아요 ④ 많아요

11 하늘에 구름이 많이 __________. 오늘은 날씨가 흐려요.

① 맑네요 ② 흐리네요 ③ 끼었네요 ④ 깨끗하네요

12 저는 샤워할 때는 반지와 귀걸이를 ________________.

① 벗어요 ② 빼요 ③ 빠져요 ④ 내려요

13 저는 감기 때문에 코가________________.

① 막혔어요 ② 복잡해요 ③ 막아요 ④ 나빠요

14 저는 취미로 매일 그림을 ____________.

① 놀아요 ② 해요 ③ 찍어요 ④ 그려요

15 남동생이 이렇게 일찍 일어나다니 해가 서쪽에서 ______________.

① 나오겠어요 ② 올라가겠어요 ③ 뜨겠어요 ④ 지겠어요

Choose the one that can replace the underlined part.

16 <u>가족</u>이 모두 몇 명이세요?

① 부모 ② 식구 ③ 형제 ④ 동생

17 저는 <u>주로</u> 도서관에서 공부해요.

① 가끔 ② 다시 ③ 매일 ④ 보통

18 저스틴은 한국어를 <u>대단히</u> 잘 해요.

① 굉장히 ② 자주 ③ 열심히 ④ 더

REVIEW Exercises

19 김 선생님은 3시에 수업을 마치세요.

① 시작하세요 ② 끝나세요 ③ 끝내세요 ④ 하세요

20 손님, 이쪽으로 오세요.

① 고객님 ② 선생님 ③ 사장님 ④ 형님

Choose the one that has the opposite meaning to the underlined part.

21 어느 지하철 역에서 내려야 해요?

① 타야 ② 세워야 ③ 올라가야 ④ 출발해야

22 요즘 날씨가 추워서 두꺼운 옷을 샀어요.

① 부드러운 ② 비싼 ③ 예쁜 ④ 얇은

23 제 새 컴퓨터는 아주 빨라요.

① 나빠요 ② 느려요 ③ 좋아요 ④ 작아요

24 어제 축구 경기에서 한국 팀이 이겼어요.

① 땄어요 ② 졌어요 ③ 떨어졌어요 ④ 넘어졌어요

25 이 식당은 아침 6시에 문을 열어요.

① 닫아요 ② 끝나요 ③ 시작해요 ④ 퇴근해요

26 선생님은 학생들의 질문에 대답했습니다.

① 답했습니다 ② 답장했습니다 ③ 물어봤습니다 ④ 받았습니다

Answer

1 ① 2 ④ 3 ① 4 ② 5 ③ 6 ② 7 ② 8 ④ 9 ② 10 ② 11 ③ 12 ② 13 ① 14 ④
15 ③ 16 ② 17 ④ 18 ① 19 ③ 20 ① 21 ① 22 ④ 23 ② 24 ② 25 ① 26 ③

LESSON 11

1 **건너편** *n.* **the opposite side**

학교 건너편에 버스 정류장이 있어요.
Across the street at the main gate of the school, there is a bus stop.

syn. 맞은편, 반대편 *n.* **the opposite side**

2 **극장(劇場) [극짱]** *n.* **theater**

오늘 학교 앞 극장에서 영화를 볼까요?
Shall we watch a movie at the movie theater in front of the school?
이번 주말에 대학로에 있는 극장에 연극을 보러 가요.
Let's go see a play at the theater on University Street.

rel. 영화관 *n.* **movie theater** ⋯▸8-15

3 **놀다** *v.* **to play; to hang out**

(ㄹ) 놀아–놉니다–놀–노는

놀러 가다 to go to play, go on an excursion,
놀러 오다 to come to play
저는 지난 주말에 친구들하고 놀았어요.
I hung out with my friends last weekend.
어제 밖에서 너무 많이 논 것 같아요.
I think I played outside too much yesterday.
이번 방학에는 뉴욕에 놀러 갈 거예요.
I will visit New York for pleasure during this break.

놀다 does not have the meaning of playing musical instruments, sports or games. Therefore, 게임을 놀다 is not a correct phrase, but you should say 게임을 하다 'to play a game.

4 **대화(對話)** *n.* **conversation, dialogue**
대화하다 *v.* **to converse**

대화를 나누다 to have a conversation
부모와 자식 사이에는 많은 대화가 필요해요.
Parents need a lot of conversations with their children.

5 **들다**[1] *v.* **to lift up, raise**

(ㄹ) 들어–듭니다–들–드는

예를 들면··· for example...

내일 파티에 올 수 있으면 손을 **드세요**.
If you can come to the party, raise your hand.

무거운 상자를 좀 **들어** 주세요. Please lift this heavy box for me.

한국의 큰 도시들로는, **예를 들면**, 서울, 부산, 대구, 인천 등이 있어요.
Big cities in Korea are, for example, Seoul, Busan, Daegu, and Incheon.

6 **만들다** *v.* **to make**

(ㄹ) 만들어–만듭니다–만들–만드는

이 음식들은 제가 다 **만들었어요**.
This food was all made by me.

제가 **만든** 노래를 들어 보세요.
Listen to the song that I made.

만들다 is not used for the following phrases: to make friends 친구를 사귀다, to make money 돈을 벌다.

7 **무겁다** *adj.* **to be heavy**

(ㅂ) 무거워–무겁습니다–무거울–무거운

이 책이 왜 이렇게 **무거워요**?
Why is this book so heavy?

가장 **무거운** 가방이 제 거예요.
The heaviest bag is mine.

ant. 가볍다 *adj.* **to be light**

8 **받다** *v.* **to receive, get, accept**

제 이메일 **받으셨어요**?
Did you receive my email?

저는 상을 **받았어요**. I received an award.

저는 오늘 고등학교때 친구한테서 전화를 **받았어요**.
I got a phone call from a high school friend.

Unlike other ㄷ–ending words such as 걷다 'to walk' (걸어요) or 듣다 'to listen to' (들어요), 받다 is not a ㄷ–irregular verb, but just a regular verb. (받아–받습니다–받을–받는)

ant. 주다 *v.* **to give** →4-18

9 **부드럽다** *adj.* **to be soft, tender, smooth**

(ㅂ) 부드러워–부드럽습니다–부드러울–부드러운

이 스테이크는 아주 **부드러워요**.
This steak is very tender.
저는 **부드러운** 목소리의 가수를 좋아해요.
I like singers with a soft voice.

ant. 딱딱하다 *adj.* **to be hard**, 거칠다 *adj.* **to be rough**

10 **사귀다** *v.* **to make friends with someone; to date someone**

사귀어–사귑니다–사귈–사귀는

저는 한국에서 한국 친구들을 많이 **사귀었어요**.
I made a lot of friends in Korea.
여자 친구랑 몇 년 **사귀었어요**?
How many years have you dated your girlfriend?

Note that the conjugated form with 어/아–beginning endings is 사귀어요 or 사귀었어요 instead of 사겨요 or 사겼어요, which are common errors found even among Korean people.

11 **서류(書類)** *n.* **document**

장학금을 신청하려면 이 **서류**들을 준비해 주세요.
If you want to apply for the scholarship, please prepare these documents.

12 **수저** *n.* **a spoon and chopsticks; spoon** →13-12

저는 엄마를 도와서 식탁에 **수저**를 놓았어요.
I helped my mom by setting spoons and chopsticks on the table.

수저 is supposed to refer to both spoons (숟가락) and chopsticks (젓가락), but it may refer to just spoons in many contexts. →13-12

13 **신청(申請)** *n.* **application; request; sign-up**
신청하다 *v.* **to apply; to sign up**

신청서 application
저는 장학금을 **신청할** 거예요. I will apply for a scholarship.
한국 비자를 받고 싶으면, 홈페이지에서 **신청서**를 다운받으세요.
If you want to receive a visa to Korea, download the application form on the Internet homepage.

14 안다 [안따]

v. **to hold, hug**

공항에서 엄마가 나를 **안아** 줬어요.
My mom gave me a hug at the airport.
제 여동생은 잘 때 곰 인형을 **안고** 자요.
My sister sleeps with a teddy bear.

15 옛날 [옌날]

n. **long time ago**

옛날 옛날에 호랑이 한 마리가 살았어요.
Once upon a time, there lived a tiger.
이 노래를 들으면 **옛날** 생각이 나요.
This song reminds me of my old days.

16 이사(移徙)
이사하다

n. **moving (of one's residence)**
v. **to move**

이삿짐센터 moving company
나는 어렸을 때, 아빠 일 때문에 **이사**를 네 번이나 했다.
When I was young, I had to move four times due to my father's job.

rel. 옮기다 *v.* **to move, shift**

17 잡다

v. **to catch, grab**

넘어지지 않게 내 손을 **잡아요**.
Hold my hand so you won't fall down.
금요일 저녁에는 택시를 **잡기가** 힘들어요.
It is hard to catch a taxi on Friday nights.

18 준비(準備)
준비하다

n. **preparation**
v. **to prepare**

다음 주에 발표가 있어서 이번 주말에 **준비해야** 돼요.
Since I have a presentation next week, I have to prepare for it this weekend.

19 **치다** *v.* **to play (tennis, piano, guitar); to hit**

운동 좋아하세요? 테니스나 골프 안 **치세요**?
Do you like sports? Don't you play tennis or golf?

저는 기타하고 피아노를 잘 **쳐요**.
I play the guitar and the piano well.

20 **행복(幸福)** *n.* **happiness**
행복하다 [행보카다] *adj.* **to be happy**

돈이 많아도 **행복하지** 못한 사람들이 많다.
There are many people who are not happy even though they have lots of money.

왕자와 공주는 결혼해서 **행복하게** 살았습니다.
The prince and the princess got married and lived happily ever after.

ant. 불행 *n.* misfortune, unhappiness

CHECK UP

건너편, 서류, 신청, 옛날, 극장, 대화, 수저, 이사, 준비, 행복

1 a spoon and chopsticks; spoon ____________

2 application; request ____________

3 conversation, dialogue ____________

4 document ____________

5 happiness ____________

6 long time ago ____________

7 moving (of one's residence) ____________

8 preparation ____________

9 the opposite side ____________

10 theater ____________

CHECK UP

만들다, 받다, 사귀다, 안다, 놀다, 들다, 무겁다, 부드럽다, 잡다, 치다

1 to be heavy ....

2 to be soft, tender, mild ....

3 to catch, grab ....

4 to hold, hug ....

5 to lift up, raise ....

6 to make ....

7 to make friends with someone; to date someone ....

8 to play (tennis, piano, guitar); to hit ....

9 to play; to hang out ....

10 to receive, get, accept ....

LESSON

12

1 **건물(建物)** *n.* **building**

고층 건물 high-rise building, skyscraper

강의실이 어느 **건물**에 있어요?
Which building is your classroom in?

서울 시내에는 **고층 건물**이 많이 있습니다.
There are many skyscrapers in downtown Seoul.

The English loanword 빌딩 specifically refers to a western style, multiple-story building, while 건물 is a more general term for building.

2 **근처(近處)** *n.* **near place; vicinity**

저는 학교 **근처**에 살아요. I live near the school.

이 **근처**에 한국 식당이 있어요?
Are there any Korean restaurants nearby?

syn. 주변 *n.* **surroundings** *n.* **nearby**

3 **놀라다** *v.* **to be surprised, startled; to be amazed**

깜짝 놀라다 to be startled all of a sudden

노아가 한국어를 너무 잘해서 모두 **놀랐어요**.
Everyone was very surprised because Noah spoke Korean very well.

풍선이 터져서 모두 **깜짝 놀랐어요**.
The balloon popped, so everyone was startled.

Be careful not to spell it 놀래다, which is a wrong form, as it is often pronounced in colloquial speech.

4 **대회(大會)** *n.* **big event, conference; (sport) competition, championship, contest**

저는 학교 테니스 **대회**에 참가할 거예요.
I am going to participate in the tennis competition at our school.

소피아는 한국어 말하기 **대회**에서 대상을 받았어요.
Sophia received the grand prize from the Korean speech contest.

5 **들다[2]** — *v.* **to cost money; take time**

(ㄹ) 들어–듭니다–
들–드는

이 숙제는 시간이 많이 **들었어요.**
This homework took a long time to do.

뉴욕에 여행가면 돈이 많이 **들** 거예요.
It will cost a lot of money to travel to New York.

들다 is generally used in the form of 시간이 들다 'take time' or 돈이 들다 'cost money'.

6 **만지다** — *v.* **to touch, pet, feel**

미술관에서 작품을 **만지면** 안 돼요.
You cannot touch the works at an art museum.

제 물건들을 **만지지** 마세요. Please don't touch my belongings.

7 **무료(無料)** — *n.* **free of charge**

무료로 for free

이번 주말에 공원에서 **무료** 공연이 있어요.
At the park this weekend, there is a free concert.

오늘은 음료수를 **무료로** 드립니다. We offer drinks for free today.

syn. 공짜 *n.* free of charge

8 **발음(發音)** — *n.* **pronunciation**
발음하다 — *v.* **to pronounce**

한국어 **발음**이 좋으시네요!
Your Korean pronunciation is really good.

이름을 정확히 **발음해** 주세요. Please pronounce your name clearly.

9 **부르다[1]** — *v.* **to call (out a person)**

(르) 불러–부릅니다–
부를–부르는

노래를 부르다 to sing a song

친구가 큰 소리로 제 이름을 **불렀어요.**
My friend called my name in a loud voice.

저는 친구들하고 자주 노래방에서 **노래를 부릅니다.**
I often sing songs with my friends at a noraebang.

10 **사다** *v.* to buy

저는 새 전화기를 **사고** 싶어요. I would like to buy a new phone.

오늘 저녁은 제가 **살게요**. I will treat you to dinner today.

ant. 팔다 *v.* to sell →23-19

11 **서점(書店)** *n.* bookstore

오늘 오후에 **서점**에서 친구를 만났어요.
I ran into my friend at a bookstore this afternoon.

서점에서 책 한 권을 샀어요. I bought a book at a bookstore.

서점 and 책방 are the most commonly used terms for referring to bookstore in general. There are some other terms that refer to bookstores such as 문고 and 서적, but they are not used independently, and are after the names of bookstores as in OO문고, XX서적.

syn. 책방 *n.* bookstore

12 **숙제(宿題) [숙쩨]** *n.* homework; assignment

숙제(를) 하다 to do one's homework

놀기 전에 **숙제**부터 다 해라.
Do all of your homework before you play.

syn. 과제 *n.* assignment, task

13 **신호등(信號燈)** *n.* traffic light

우리 학교 앞에 있는 **신호등**이 고장나서 지금 차가 많이 막혀요.
Because the traffic lights in front of my school are not working, the traffic is congested now.

Green light in 신호등 is often called 파란불, because 파란색 sometimes refers to "green" in Korean culture. Red lights and yellow lights are 빨간불, and 노란불 respectively.

14 **안부(安否)** *n.* regards, news on whether someone is fine

–에게 안부를 전하다 to give regards to,

–의 안부를 묻다 to ask/inquire after somebody

한국에 가면 김 선생님께 제 **안부** 좀 전해 주세요.
When you go to Korea, please give my regards to Prof. Kim.

15 오래 — *adv.* **for a long while**

오래간만 after a long while (=오랜만), 오랫동안 for a long time

집에서 학교까지 **오래** 걸려요.
It takes a long time from my house to my school.

잘 지내셨어요? 정말 **오래간만**이에요.
How have you been? It's been really a long time.

16 이야기하다 — *v.* **to talk, chat**

저는 엄마한테 전화해서 밤 늦게까지 **이야기했어요**.
I called my mom and talked with her until late at night.

In colloquial speech, it is usually contracted as 얘기하다.
늦은 밤에는 조용히 **얘기하세요**. Please talk softly late at night.

rel. 말하다 *v.* **to speak** ⋯ 14-6

17 잡지(雜誌) [잡찌] — *n.* **magazine, journal**

나는 한국어 공부를 위해 신문이나 **잡지**를 자주 본다.
To study Korean, I often read newspapers or magazines.

rel. 신문 *n.* **newspaper**

18 중요하다(重要–) — *adj.* **to be important, significant**

성공을 위해 가장 **중요한** 것은 인간 관계입니다.
The most important thing for success is human relationships.

저는 제 가족이 제일 **중요해요**. For me, my family is most important.

19 친구(親舊) — *n.* **friend**

친구를 사귀다 to make friends ⋯ 11-10, 가장/제일 친한 친구 the best friend

노아는 한국 **친구**가 아주 많아요. Noah has a lot of Korean friends.

20 현금(現金) — *n.* **cash**

요즘은 **현금**보다 신용 카드를 더 많이 쓰고 있다.
Nowadays people are using credit cards more than cash.

rel. 신용카드 *n.* **credit card**

CHECK UP

건물, 무료, 서점, 신호등, 오래, 잡지, 친구, 근처, 대회, 안부, 현금

1 bookstore ____________________

2 building ____________________

3 for a long time ____________________

4 free of charge ____________________

5 friend ____________________

6 magazine, journal ____________________

7 traffic light ____________________

8 big event, conference; ____________________

9 cash ____________________

10 near place; vicinity ____________________

11 regards, news on whether someone is fine ____________________

CHECK UP

만지다, 사다, 이야기하다, 중요하다, 놀라다, 들다,
부르다, 숙제하다, 발음하다

1 to be important, significant ....

2 to be surprised, startled; to be amazed ....

3 to buy ....

4 to call (out a person) ....

5 to cost money; take time ....

6 to do homework ....

7 to pronounce ....

8 to talk, chat ....

9 to touch, pat, feel ....

Describing Taste

Choose the word that best fills in the blank. Please conjugate it appropriately.

맵다, 짜다, 시다, 쓰다, 달다, 싱겁다

1. 국에 소금을 많이 넣어서 너무 ________.
2. 소금이 많이 들어간 ________ 음식은 건강에 안 좋아요.
3. 음식에 식초를 많이 넣어서 너무 ________.
4. 레몬이나 라임은 ________ 맛이 강해요.
5. 이 초콜릿에는 설탕이 안 들어갔어요. 그래서 맛이 아주 ________.
6. 이 커피는 너무 진해요. 저는 맛이 너무 ________ 커피는 싫어해요.
7. 비빔밥에 고추장을 너무 많이 넣어서 아주 ________.
8. 한국 음식에는 고춧가루가 많이 들어간 ________ 음식이 많아요.
9. 이 케이크에는 설탕이 너무 많이 들어 있어서 ________.
10. 초콜릿, 케이크, 사탕처럼 ________ 음식을 많이 먹으면 살이 쪄요.
11. 이 음식에는 소금이 적게 들어가서 좀 ________.
12. 저희 할아버지는 보통 소금이 안 들어간 ________ 음식을 드세요.

Answer

1 짜요 **2** 짠 **3** 시어요/셔요 **4** 신 **5** 써요 **6** 쓴 **7** 매워요 **8** 매운 **9** 달아요 **10** 단 **11** 싱거워요 **12** 싱거운

LESSON

13

1 **걷다** *v.* **to walk**

(ㄷ) 걸어 – 걷습니다 – 걸을 – 걷는

걸어가다 to go on foot, 걸어오다 to come on foot

저는 학교에 **걸어서** 왔어요. I came to school on foot.

저희 아버지는 매일 공원에서 **걸으세요**.
My father walks at the park every day.

rel. 뛰다 *v.* to run; to jump 24-5, 달리다 *v.* to run 1-4

2 **금년(今年)** *n.* **this year**

금년 겨울은 따뜻할 거예요. This winter is going to be warm.

Note that 이 년 does not make sense.

syn. 올해, 이번 해 this year, *rel.* 내년 next year, 작년 last year

3 **높다** *adj.* **to be high**

서울에서 어느 건물이 제일 **높아요**?
What is the highest building in Seoul?

오늘은 기온이 **높겠습니다**. Today's temperature is going to be high.

ant. 낮다 *adj.* to be low 4-3

4 **더럽다** *adj.* **to be dirty**

(ㅂ) 더러워 – 더럽습니다 – 더러울 – 더러운

옷이 너무 **더러워요**. 빨아야겠어요.
These clothes are too dirty. You need to wash them.

저 **더러운** 옷들을 오늘 꼭 빨 거예요.
I will definitely wash those dirty clothes.

ant. 깨끗하다 *adj.* to be clean 19-2

5 **들리다** *v.* **to be heard, be audible**

제 목소리가 **들리세요**? Can you hear my voice?

들리다 is a passive form of 듣다 'to hear' here.

6 **많다 [만타]** *adj.* **to be many, much**
많이 [마니] *adv.* **much, lot**

오늘은 할 일이 **많아요**. There are lots of things to do today.

많은 학생들이 한국어를 공부하고 있어요.
Many students are studying Korean.

오늘 저녁을 **많이** 먹어서 벌써 졸려요.
Since I had a big dinner, I am already sleepy.

Note that 많은 is followed by a noun, while 많이 should be followed by a verb or adjective.

ant. 적다 *adj.* **(amount) to be few; to be little** → 15-7

7 **무섭다** *adj.* **to be scary; to be scared of**

(ㅂ) 무서워 - 무섭습니다 - 무서울 - 무서운

옆집 할아버지는 좀 **무서우세요**.
The old man next door is very scary.

저는 뱀이 너무 **무서워요**. I am very scared of snakes.

저는 **무서운** 영화를 좋아해요. I like scary movies.

8 **발표(發表)** *n.* **presentation, announcement**
발표하다 *v.* **to announce, make a presentation**

다음 주 수업 시간에 한국 문화에 대해서 **발표**를 할 거예요.
I am going to present about Korean culture in class next week.

9 **부르다**[2] *adj.* **to be bulged out, full**

(르) 불러 - 부릅니다 - 부를 - 부르는

배가 **부르다** to have eaten one's fill; to be full

저는 너무 배가 **불러서** 졸려요. I am sleepy because I am too full.

ant. 배(가) 고프다 *adj.* **to be hungry**

10 **사랑** *n.* **love**
사랑하다 *v.* **to love**

사랑에 빠지다 to fall in love

저는 친구들의 **사랑**을 많이 받았어요.
I have been loved by many friends of mine.

제가 제일 **사랑하는** 사람은 우리 엄마예요.
The person that I love the most is my mom.

11 **선물(膳物)** *n.* **gift, present**

선물 가게 gift shop

저는 친구 생일 **선물**을 사러 백화점에 갈 거예요.

I will go to the department store to buy a birthday present for my friend.

12 **숟가락 [숟까락]** *n.* **spoon** ···› Appendix D

한국에서는 밥은 **숟가락**, 반찬은 젓가락으로 먹어야 해요.

In Korea, you are supposed to use spoons for rice and chopsticks for side dishes.

rel. 수저 *n.* spoon and chopsticks; (sometimes) spoon ···› 11-12, 젓가락 *n.* chopsticks

13 **실수(失手) [실쑤]** *n.* **mistake**
실수하다 *v.* **to make a mistake**

실수로 by mistake

선생님, 제가 **실수로** 숙제를 안 가지고 왔어요.

Teacher, by mistake, I did not bring my homework.

제가 **실수했네요**. 미안해요.

I made a mistake. Sorry.

14 **앉다 [안따]** *v.* **to sit**

다리가 아프면 의자에 좀 **앉아** 계세요.

If your legs hurt, please have a seat for a while.

rel. 서다 *v.* to stand ···› 9-11, 눕다 *v.* to lie down

15 **오르다** *v.* **to climb, increase**

(르) 올라 – 오릅니다 – 오를 – 오르는

올라가다 *v.* to go up, 올라오다 *v.* to come up

우리 학교의 학비가 매년 **오릅니다**.

The tuition of my school increases every year.

소피아는 2층에 있다. **올라가** 봐라.

Sophia is on the second floor. Why don't you go up?

16 인사(人事) — *n.* greeting, salutation, bow
인사하다 — *v.* to greet, give a bow

옆집 아이는 사람들에게 **인사**를 잘한다.
The kid next door is good with greeting people.

rel. 절 *n.* (Korean style formal) deep bow, 절하다 *v.* to bow

17 장소(場所) — *n.* location

내일 만날 시간과 **장소**를 알려 주세요.
Please let me know when and where we will meet tomorrow.

18 즐겁다 — *adj.* to be pleasant, joyful

(ㅂ) 즐거워-
즐겁습니다-
즐거울- 즐거운

작년 여름에 친구들하고 여행할 때 정말 **즐거웠어요**.
I was really overjoyed when I traveled with my friends last summer.

즐거운 시간 보내세요! Have a great time!

19 친절하다(親切-) — *adj.* to be kind, friendly, considerate

주인 아저씨가 **친절해서** 학교 앞 식당에 자주 가요.
I go to the restaurant in front of my school because the owner is kind.

ant. 불친절하다 *adj.* to be unkind, unfriendly

20 혼자 — *n./adv.* alone

저는 룸메이트가 없어요. 방을 **혼자** 써요.
I don't have a roommate. I use my room by myself.

힘 내. 넌 **혼자**가 아니야. Cheer up. You are not alone.

CHECK UP

금년, 발표, 사랑, 선물, 숟가락, 실수, 인사, 장소, 혼자

1 alone ____________

2 greeting, bow ____________

3 location ____________

4 love ____________

5 mistake ____________

6 present, gift ____________

7 presentation, announcement ____________

8 spoon ____________

9 this year ____________

CHECK UP

걷다, 높다, 더럽다, 들리다, 많다, 무섭다, 부르다, 앉다, 오르다, 즐겁다, 친절하다

1 to be dirty ______________________

2 to be full, bulged out ______________________

3 to be heard, audible ______________________

4 to be high ______________________

5 to be kind, considerate ______________________

6 to be many, much ______________________

7 to be pleasant ______________________

8 to be scary ______________________

9 to climb, increase ______________________

10 to sit ______________________

11 to walk ______________________

Verbs for "Wear"

Choose the word that best fills in the blank. Please conjugate it appropriately. ⋯› Appendix N and O

입다, 신다, 쓰다, 끼다, 매다, 차다, 하다

1 수업 시간에 모자를 __________ 안 돼요.

2 우리 반에는 안경을 __________ 사람들이 많아요.

3 이 반지를 한번 __________ 보세요.

4 저는 편한 옷을 좋아해서 매일 청바지를 __________.

5 제 친구는 오늘 예쁜 목걸이를 __________

6 저는 눈이 나빠서 콘택트 렌즈를 __________.

7 운동할 때에는 양말을 꼭 __________.

8 내일은 운동화를 __________ 오세요.

9 오늘 인터뷰가 있어서 넥타이를 __________왔어요.

10 오토바이를 탈 때 헬멧을 꼭 __________.

11 차를 탈 때는 꼭 안전벨트를 __________.

12 저는 보통 시계를 잘 안 __________.

13 제 언니는 매일 아침 화장을 __________.

14 오늘은 추우니까 꼭 장갑을 __________.

15 소피아는 오늘 예쁜 티셔츠를 __________.

Answer

1 쓰면 2 낀/쓴 3 끼어/껴 4 입어요 5 했어요 6 끼어요/껴요 7 신어요 8 신고 9 매고 10 쓰세요 11 매세요/하세요 12 차요 13 해요 14 끼세요 15 입었어요

LESSON 14

1 **걸리다[1]** *v.* **to be caught**

병/감기에 걸리다 to get sick/cold → 4-9

저는 눈병에 **걸려서** 학교에 안 갔어요.
I got an eye disease, so I didn't go to school.

ant. 낫다 *v.* **to recover (from an illness)**

2 **기다리다** *v.* **to wait for**

소현이가 약속에 늦었어요. 그래서 저는 소현이를 30분 동안 **기다렸어요**.
Sohyeon was late for our appointment. So I waited for her for 30 minutes.

잠깐만 **기다리세요**. Wait a second, please.

3 **놓다 [노타]** *v.* **to lay, put something down; to release, let go**

종업원이 테이블에 음식을 **놓고** 갔어요.
The waiter put the food on the table and left.

노아는 잡은 물고기를 **놓아** 주었습니다.
Noah released the fish that he had caught.

4 **덕분(德分) [덕뿐]** *n.* **favor**

~ 덕분에 thanks to ~, by someone's favor

저는 친구 **덕분에** 숙제를 끝낼 수 있었어요.
I could finish my homework thanks to my friend.

덕분에 잘 지내고 있습니다. Thanks to you, I am doing well.

5 **들어가다** *v.* **to enter; to go in**

들어오다 to come in

가: **들어가도** 돼요? May I come in?

나: 네, **들어오세요**! Yes, come on in!

6 **말** *n.* **words, speech**
말하다 *v.* **to speak**

내 **말** 좀 들어 봐요. Please listen to what I'm saying.

아기가 **말**을 배우고 있어요. The baby is learning how to speak.

말하다 vs. 이야기하다 → 12-16

말하다 focuses on the action of speaking, while 이야기하다 'to tell' focuses more on the contents of the speech.

우리 개가 말을 할 수 있었으면 좋겠어요.
I wish that my dog could speak.

할머니가 재미있는 옛날 **이야기**를 해 주셨어요.
My grandmother told me an interesting old story.

The honorific form of 말 is 말씀.

선생님이 **말씀** 하실 때는 잘 들으세요.
When the teacher is speaking, please listen carefully.

말씀 can also be a humble form of 말. Thus, when a socially lower person talks to a socially higher person, 말씀 should be used instead of 말 as in 저는 선생님께 내일 학교에 못 온다고 **말씀**드렸어요. I told my teacher that I cannot come to school tomorrow.

7 **무역(貿易)** *n.* **trade**

국제 무역 international trade

저는 **무역** 회사에서 일하고 싶어요. I want to work at a trading company.

8 **밝다 [박따]** *adj.* **to be bright**

이 방은 **밝아요**. This room is bright.

요즘은 **밝은**색 옷이 유행이에요.
These days, bright clothes are in fashion.

현우 씨는 성격이 **밝아서** 좋아요.
Hyeonwu's personality is bright, which is good.

ant. 어둡다 *adj.* **to be dark**

9 **부모(父母)** *n.* **parents**

우리는 **부모님**께 효도해야 돼요. We have to be filial to our parents.

The words like 부모, 선생 'teacher', and 교수 'professor', which refer to respectable entity are usually followed by the honorific title suffix –님 as in 부모님, 선생님 'teacher', and 교수님 'professor'.

10 **사무실(事務室)** *n.* **office (room)**

오늘 오후에는 제가 **사무실**에 있을 거예요. 이따가 연락하세요.
I am going to be in my office this afternoon. Contact me a little later.

For professors' office, 연구실 'research room' is generally used, while 사무실 usually refers to department offices or other offices.

11 **선배(先輩)** *n.* a senior member at school or work place

한국에서는 **선배**한테 인사를 잘 해야 해요.
In Korea, you have to greet your senior members politely.

선배 can be used as a title after one's name (first, last or full name). For example, if your friend 김준수 is your senior member, you can call him 김선배, 준수 선배, or 김준수 선배. However, 후배 'junior' is not usually used for addressing people.

ant. 후배 *n.* junior member at school or work place

12 **숫자(數字) [숟짜]** *n.* number

비밀번호에는 알파벳과 **숫자**가 다 있어야 해요.
The password must include both alphabets and numbers.

13 **싫다 [실타]** *adj.* to be unpleasant; not likable

저는 뱀이 **싫어요**. I hate snakes.

저는 아침에 일찍 일어나는 것이 **싫어요**.
I hate waking up early in the morning.

Note that 싫다 is an adjective, so it cannot take any object. So "저는 뱀을 싫어요" is a grammatically wrong sentence.

ant. 좋다 *adj.* to be likable →3-18, *rel.* 싫어하다 *v.* to dislike

14 **않다 [안타]** *v.* to not be, to not do

지난 주에는 많이 바빴는데 이번 주에는 바쁘지 **않아요**.
I was very busy last week, but I am not that busy this week.

저는 고기는 먹지 **않아요**. I don't eat meat.

Used in the form of '~지 않다' after a verb or an adjective to negate it. This is a long-negation form, while '안 + Verb/Adj' is a short-negation form.

오늘은 춥지 않아요 = 오늘은 안 추워요. It is not cold today.

15 **외국(外國)** *n.* foreign country

외국어 foreign language, 외국인 foreigner

저는 우리 나라에서는 여행을 많이 다녔는데, **외국** 여행은 이번이 처음이에요.
I have traveled a lot throughout my country, but this is my first trip abroad.

16 일
일하다

n. work
v. to work

아버지가 할 **일**이 너무 많아서 집에 늦게 오셨어요.
My father came home late because there was too much work to do.
어디에서 **일하고** 싶어요? Where do you want to work?

When you go to work, we don't generally say 일에 가다 although we can say 일하러 가다, 직장에 가다, or 회사에 가다. (직장 workplace, 회사 company)

rel. 아르바이트 *n.* part-time job

17 재미없다

adj. to be no fun, to be boring

가: 어제 본 영화 어땠어요? 재미있었어요?
How was the movie you watched yesterday? Was it funny?
나: 아니요, **재미없었어요**. 보지 마세요.
No, it was not funny. Don't watch it.

ant. 재미있다 *adj.* to be fun

18 지금(只今)

n./adv. now

지금 몇 시예요? What time is it now?
저는 **지금** 카페에서 책 읽고 있어요.
Right now, I'm reading a book at a café.

19 친하다(親-)

adj. to be close, intimate

저는 소현이하고 아주 **친해요**. I am close to Sohyeon.
소현이는 저하고 제일 **친한** 친구예요. Sohyeon is my best friend.

rel. 친절하다 *adj.* to be kind, friendly ⋯ 13-19

20 화(火)

n. anger, rage

화가 나다 to be angry, 화를 내다 to get angry (*lit.* to express one's anger)
옆집 사람이 너무 시끄러워서 **화가 났어요**.
I was really angry because my neighbor was too noisy.
학생들이 숙제를 안 해서 선생님이 **화를 내셨어요**.
Because the students didn't do their homework, our teacher got angry.

CHECK UP

덕분, 말, 무역, 부모, 사무실, 선배, 숫자, 외국, 일, 지금, 화

1 favor ____________

2 anger ____________

3 foreign country ____________

4 now ____________

5 number ____________

6 office ____________

7 parents ____________

8 senior member ____________

9 trade ____________

10 words, speech ____________

11 work ____________

CHECK UP

걸리다, 기다리다, 놓다, 들어가다, 밝다, 싫다, 않다, 재미없다, 친하다

1 to be caught ______________________

2 to be bright ______________________

3 to be close ______________________

4 to be no fun, boring ______________________

5 to be unpleasant ______________________

6 to enter ______________________

7 to not be, to not do ______________________

8 to put something down; release ______________________

9 to wait for ______________________

Verbs for "Play"

Choose the word that best fills in the blank. Please conjugate it appropriately.

치다, 켜다, 하다, 불다

1. 저는 취미로 피아노를 ________.
2. 제 동생은 바이올린을 잘 ________.
3. 저는 어렸을 때 매일 야구를 ________.
4. 학생들이 운동장에서 축구를 ________.
5. 저하고 같이 배드민턴을 ________?
6. 저는 동생하고 같이 탁구를 ________.
7. 아버지는 주말에 골프를 ________.
8. 저희 누나는 플루트를 잘 ________.
9. 학생들이 PC방에서 컴퓨터 게임을 ________.
10. 옆집에서 어떤 사람이 드럼을 ________. 너무 시끄러워요.
11. 주말에 저하고 같이 테니스를 ________?
12. 저는 고등학교 때 배구를 좋아해서 매일 배구를 ________.

Answer

1 쳐요 **2** 켜요/해요 **3** 했어요 **4** 해요 **5** 칠래요/칠까요 **6** 쳐요 **7** 치세요 **8** 불어요 **9** 해요 **10** 쳐요 **11** 칠래요/칠까요? **12** 했어요

LESSON 15

1 **걸리다²** *v.* **to take time**

집에서 학교까지 걸어서 20분쯤 **걸려요**.
From my house to school, it takes about 20 minutes by foot.
이 숙제 끝내는 데에 시간이 많이 **걸렸어요**.
It took me a long time to finish this homework.

2 **기분(氣分)** *n.* **feeling**

기분이 좋다 to feel good, be in a good mood,
기분이 나쁘다 to feel bad, be in a bad mood
선생님께 칭찬을 들어서 **기분이 좋아요**.
I was praised by my teacher so I felt good.

기분이 나쁘다 'to feel bad' does not generally mean 'to feel sick'. For feeling bad due to sickness, 몸이 안 좋다 should be used.

3 **늦다** *v.* **to be delayed; to be late**

늦게 *adv.* late
오늘 저는 수업에 **늦었어요**. I was late for class.
제 친구는 언제나 약속시간에 **늦게** 와요.
My friend always comes late for our appointments.
오늘 아침에는 **늦게** 일어났어요. I got up late this morning.

Note that 늦다 is a verb, so its present noun modifying form is **늦는**: 수업에 매일 **늦는** 사람이 누구예요? Who is the person who is late for the class everyday?

4 **덜** *adv.* **less; incompletely**

제 비빔밥은 **덜** 맵게 해 주세요.
Please make my bibimbap less spicy.
일이 아직 **덜** 끝났어요. The work is not finished yet.

ant. 더 *adv.* more

5 **말다** *v.* **to stop, cease; not … but …**

(ㄹ) 말아 – 맙니다 – 말 – 마는

여기서는 담배를 피우지 **마세요**. Please don't smoke here.
도서관에서는 놀지 **말고** 공부하세요. Don't play, but study at the library.
~말고 not ~ (but ~)
이거 **말고** 저거 주세요. Not this one, but give me that one, please.

말다 is not used independently, but used in the form of ~지 말다, ~지 말고~ after a verb as shown in the above examples.

6 무용(舞踊) *n.* **(classical) dance, dancing**

무용가 dancer

저는 현대 **무용**을 전공하고 있어요. I am majoring in modern dance.

syn. 춤 *n.* dance → 8-19

7 방(房) *n.* **room**

제 **방**에는 침대하고 책상, 옷장, 책장이 있어요.
In my room, there is a bed, desk, closet and bookshelf.

호텔에 빈 **방**이 없어서 예약을 못 했어요.
There was no vacant room at the hotel, so I couldn't reserve any.

Many business places end with -방: 찜질방 Korean dry sauna, 노래방 Korean karaoke, PC방 Internet cafe, 빨래방 laundromat.

8 부부(夫婦) *n.* **married couple, husband and wife**

신혼부부 newly married couple

이 운동은 **부부**가 같이 하면 좋아요.
This exercise is good for a married couple to do together.

9 사업(事業) *n.* **business**
사업하다 [사어파다] *v.* **to do business**

사업가 business man

저는 졸업 후에 **사업**을 하고 싶어요.
I want to do business after I graduate.

10 산책(散策) *n.* **walk, stroll**
산책하다 [산채카다] *v.* **to take a walk**

산책로 trail

저희 할아버지는 매일 아침에 **산책**을 하세요.
My grandfather takes a walk every morning.

11 **선수(選手)** *n.* **athlete, player**

운동 선수 sports player, athlete

야구는 한 팀에 아홉 명의 **선수**가 경기를 해요.

For baseball, nine players on each team play the game.

12 **쉬다** *v.* **to take a rest; to take a day off**

쉬어 - 쉽니다 - 쉴 - 쉬는

쉬는 시간 recess

피곤하시지요? 오늘 밤에는 푹 **쉬세요**.

You must be tired. Please take a good rest tonight.

감기에 걸려서 학교를 하루 **쉬었어요**.

Because I caught a cold, I had a day off of school.

13 **심심하다** *adj.* **to be bored (because there is nothing interesting to do)**

현우야, 우리 **심심한데** 영화나 보러 갈까?

Hyeonwu, I'm so bored. Do you want to go to the movies with me?

The subject of 심심하다 should be a person or an animal. If an event is boring, 재미없다 or 지루하다 should be appropriate. 이 영화는 너무 지루해요. 'This movie is very boring.'

14 **알다** *v.* **to know**

(ㄹ) 알아 - 압니다 - 알 - 아는

저는 아직 1학년이라서 학교에 **아는** 사람이 별로 없어요.

Because I am still a freshman, I don't know many people on campus.

~(으)ㄹ 줄 알다 means 'to know how to ~' and it is used to talk about one's ability of doing something.

저는 운전을 **할 줄 알아요**. I know how to drive.

ant. 모르다 *v.* **to not know** ···4-7

15 **외식하다(外食–) [외시카다]** *v.* **to eat out**

오늘은 엄마 생일이에요. 오늘 저녁에 가족하고 **외식할 거예요**.

Today is my mom's birthday. I'm going to eat out with my family tonight.

16 일기(日記) *n.* **journal, diary**

소피아는 거의 매일 밤에 일기를 쓴다.
Sophia writes in her diary almost every night.

17 적다 *adj.* **to be few, little**

적어도 at least

밥이 너무 적어요. 조금 더 주세요.
The rice is too little. Please give me some more.

적은 돈으로도 행복하게 살 수 있어요.
Even with little money, you can live happily.

ant. 많다 *adj.* **to be many, much** ··· 13-6,
rel. 작다 *adj.* **to be small (in size)** ··· 6-17

18 지난 *adj.* **last**

지나다 to pass, go by

지난 달 last month, 지난 번 last time, 지난 주 last week

이번 주 날씨는 지난 주보다 따뜻하겠습니다.
It will be warmer this week compare to last week.

ant. 다음 *n.* **next, following** ··· 20-3

19 침대(寢臺) *n.* **bed** ··· Appendix K

저는 오늘 아침 10시까지 침대에 누워 있었어요.
I was lying down on my bed until 10 o'clock this morning.

Korean expression for English phrase "go to bed/sleep" is 자러 가다: 이제 자러 갈 시간이에요. 'It's time to go to bed.'

20 화장(化粧) *n.* **make-up**
화장하다 *v.* **to wear makeup**

화장품 cosmetics

오늘 저녁에 파티가 있어요. 집에서 화장 좀 하고 올게요.
I have a party tonight. I will go home to put on some makeup.

CHECK UP

기분, 덜, 무용, 방, 부부, 사업, 선수, 일기, 침대, 화장

1 feeling ....

2 athlete, player ....

3 bed ....

4 business ....

5 dance ....

6 husband and wife ....

7 journal, diary ....

8 less, incompletely ....

9 make-up ....

10 room ....

CHECK UP

걸리다, 늦다, 말다, 산책하다, 쉬다, 심심하다, 알다, 외식하다, 적다, 지난

1 last ....

2 to be bored ....

3 to be delayed, late ....

4 to be few, little ....

5 to eat out ....

6 to know ....

7 to stop, cease ....

8 to take a rest ....

9 to take time ....

10 to take a walk ....

REVIEW Exercises

Choose the one which is most appropriate in the blank.

1 저는 한국 친구들을 많이 __________ 싶어요.

① 만들고 ② 사귀고 ③ 이야기하고 ④ 놀고

2 저는 제 여자 친구하고 2년 동안 __________.

① 사귀었어요 ② 만들었어요 ③ 사귀어요 ④ 만들어요

3 제 남동생은 매일 컴퓨터로 게임을 __________.

① 봐요 ② 놀아요 ③ 쳐요 ④ 해요

4 제 동생은 피아노를 잘 __________.

① 해요 ② 놀아요 ③ 쳐요 ④ 켜요

5 저는 친구들하고 어제 노래방에서 두 시간 동안 노래를 __________.

① 불었어요 ② 불렀어요 ③ 부었어요 ④ 부르세요

6 서울에 가면 김선생님께 안부 좀 ________ 주세요.

① 전해 ② 보내 ③ 들어 ④ 드려

7 소피아는 제 ______________ 친구예요.

① 제일 ② 제일 친한 ③ 가장 ④ 친절한

8 오늘 점심을 안 먹었어요. 그래서 지금 아주 __________.

① 배가 고파요 ② 배가 불러요 ③ 맛있어요 ④ 요리해요

9 저는 룸메이트가 없어요. 그래서 방을 __________ 쓰고 있어요.

① 같이 ② 둘이서 ③ 혼자 ④ 함께

10 저는 감기에 __________ 학교에 못 갔어요.

① 걸어서 ② 아파서 ③ 걸려서 ④ 되어서

11 종업원이 테이블에 음식을 __________ 갔어요.

① 넣고 ② 가지고 ③ 눕고 ④ 놓고

12 친구가 숙제를 도와줬어요. 친구 __________ 숙제를 빨리 했어요.

① 고마워서 ② 덕분에 ③ 같이 ④ 보다

13 수업 시간에는 선생님 __________을/를 잘 들으세요.

① 교과서 ② 수업 ③ 말씀 ④ 소리

14 옆집 사람이 너무 시끄러워서 너무 화가 __________.

① 내렸어요 ② 냈어요 ③ 나왔어요 ④ 났어요

15 큰 소리가 나서 모두 __________ 놀랐어요.

① 깜짝 ② 별로 ③ 늘 ④ 갑자기

Choose the one that can replace the underlined part.

16 학교 정문 <u>건너편</u>에 버스 정류장이 있어요.

① 저편 ② 사이 ③ 거기 ④ 맞은편

17 이 <u>근방</u>에 맛있는 한국 음식이 있어요?

① 방금 ② 이웃 ③ 근처 ④ 금방

18 오늘은 음료수를 <u>공짜로</u> 드립니다.

① 무료로 ② 세일로 ③ 선물로 ④ 더

REVIEW Exercises

19 오늘 오후에는 학교앞 책방에서 책을 살 거예요.

① 책집 ② 상점 ③ 문구점 ④ 서점

20 금년 겨울은 따뜻하네요!

① 내년 ② 올해 ③ 지난 해 ④ 다음 해

Choose the one that has the opposite meaning to the underlined part.

21 이 케이크는 아주 부드러워요. 너무 맛있네요!

① 무거워요 ② 딱딱해요 ③ 가벼워요 ④ 약해요

22 이 가방은 왜 이렇게 무거워요?

① 가벼워요 ② 딱딱해요 ③ 커요 ④ 부드러워요

23 저는 백화점에서 새 신발을 사고 싶어요

① 보고 ② 구경하고 ③ 팔고 ④ 벗고

24 한국에서는 선배한테 인사를 잘 해야 돼요.

① 선생 ② 후배 ③ 동생 ④ 학생

25 저는 주말에 일찍 일어나는 것이 정말 싫어요.

① 사랑해요 ② 기뻐해요 ③ 좋아해요 ④ 좋아요

26 서울에서 어떤 건물이 제일 높아요?

① 짧아요 ② 낮아요 ③ 커요 ④ 작아요

Answer

1 ② 2 ① 3 ④ 4 ③ 5 ② 6 ① 7 ② 8 ① 9 ③ 10 ③ 11 ④ 12 ② 13 ③ 14 ④
15 ① 16 ④ 17 ③ 18 ① 19 ④ 20 ② 21 ② 22 ① 23 ③ 24 ② 25 ④ 26 ②

LESSON

16

1 **결혼 (結婚)**
결혼하다

n. **marriage**
v. **to get married**

결혼식 wedding ceremony

저는 여자 친구하고 내년에 **결혼**을 **할** 거예요.
I will marry my girlfriend next year.

저랑 **결혼해** 주실래요? Will you marry me?

결혼하다 cannot directly take an object as in English, but requires a particle such as 하고, 와/과, or (이)랑 'with' as shown in the above examples.

ant. 이혼 *n.* **divorce** *rel.* 약혼하다 *v.* **to be engaged**

2 **기숙사(寄宿舍)**
[기숙싸]

n. **dormitory**

우리 학교에서는 1학년 때는 **기숙사**에 살아야 돼요. In our school, you have to live in the dorm during your freshman year.

3 **다니다**

v. **to go (and attend) regularly**

제 여동생은 고등학교에 **다녀요**.
My younger sister goes to high school.

The place you go to should be followed by 에, so the structure should be ~에 다니다.

It may compose complex verbs such as 놀러 다니다 'to play about' or 걸어 다니다 'to walk around, walk about'

고등학교 때 저는 친구들하고 매일 놀러 다녔어요.
In my high school days, I played around with my friends everyday.

공원에는 많은 사람들이 걸어 다니고 있어요.
Many people are walking around the park.

4 **덥다**

(ㅂ) 더워 – 덥습니다 – 더울 – 더운

adj. **(weather) to be hot**

무덥다 to be sweltering, muggy

서울의 여름은 너무 **더워요**. The summers in Seoul are too hot.

오늘같이 **더운** 날에는 밖에서 운동하기 싫어요.
On a hot day like today, I don't want to exercise outside.

덥다 is mostly used for describing air temperature or weather. For foods or drinking water, 뜨겁다 should be used.

ant. 춥다 *adj.* (weather) to be cold ⋯9-19

5 **따뜻하다 [따뜨타다]** *adj.* to be mild, warm; to be kind

이번 겨울은 작년보다 **따뜻해요.**
This winter is warmer than last year.
우리 선생님은 무섭게 생기셨지만 마음이 **따뜻하세요.**
My teacher looks scary, but he has a kind heart.

rel. 쌀쌀하다 *adj.* (weather) to be cold, chilly

6 **맑다 [막따]** *adj.* to be clear, pure

이 호수는 물이 **맑아서** 바닥까지 다 보여요.
This lake is so clear that we can see the bottom.
어제는 비가 왔는데 오늘은 날씨가 **맑아요.**
It rained yesterday, but it is clear today.

ant. 흐리다 *adj.* to be unclear; to be overcast ⋯23-20

7 **무척** *adv.* very, really, extremely

어제는 **무척** 더운 날이었어요. It was a very hot day yesterday.

syn. 매우 *adv.* very much ⋯18-6, 굉장히 *adv.* very, immensely ⋯2-2

8 **방금(方今)** *adv.* just now

열차가 **방금** 떠났습니다. The train has just left.

방금 vs. 금방

금방 may be used as a synonym of 방금 as in '열차가 금방 떠났어요.' but in most contexts, it is used to refer to 'in a short while, shortly' as follows: 금방 돌아올게요. I'll come back soon.

rel. 아까 *adv.* a while ago ⋯2-14

9 **부지런하다** *adj.* to be hard working, diligent

저희 어머니는 참 **부지런하세요.** 매일 일찍 일어나서 운동을 하세요.
My mother is very hard-working. She wakes up early and exercises every day.

10 **사용하다(使用-)** *v.* **to use, make use of**

2층 화장실은 오늘 **사용하지** 마세요.
Don't use the restroom on the second floor today.
우리 선생님은 수업에서 비디오를 자주 **사용하세요.**
My teacher often uses videos in class.

syn. 쓰다 *v.* **to use** 24-12, 이용하다 *v.* **to make use of**

11 **선택하다(選擇-)** *v.* **to choose**
[선태카다]
선택 *n.* **choice**

작년에 여러 학교에 가 보고 우리 학교를 **선택했어요.**
I visited many schools last year and selected my school.
제 **선택**을 믿어 보세요. Please trust my choice.

12 **쉽다** *adj.* **to be easy**

(ㅂ) 쉬워-
쉽습니다-쉬운-쉬울

한글은 배우기 **쉬워요.**
Hangeul (the Korean writing system) is easy to learn.

ant. 어렵다 *adj.* **to be difficult**

13 **심하다(甚-)** *adj.* **to be serious, severe, harsh**

현우는 감기가 **심해서** 학교에 못 갔어요.
Hyeonwu caught a severe cold, so he could not go to school.
소현이는 너무 **심한** 농담에 기분이 나빠졌습니다.
Sohyeon felt bad when she heard a harsh joke.

14 **약(藥)** *n.* **medicine**

약을 먹다 to take medicine, 약을 바르다 to apply ointment/liquid medicine, 약사 pharmacist, 약국 pharmacy
머리가 아파서 **약을 먹었어요.**
Because I had a headache, I took some medicine.
미안하지만 **약국**에 가서 감기**약** 좀 사 주세요.
I am sorry, but please buy me some cold medicine at the pharmacy.

15 외출하다(外出 –)
외출

v. **to go out**
n. **going out**

가: 오늘 집에 계실 거예요? Are you going to stay at home today?
나: 아니요, 잠깐 **외출할** 거예요. No, I'm going to go out for a while.

16 일기예보(日氣豫報)

n. **weather forecast**

아침에 **일기예보**를 안 봐서 우산을 안 가지고 왔어요.
Because I did not watch the weather forecast, I didn't bring an umbrella.

rel. 날씨 *n.* weather → 3-3

17 전공(專攻)
전공하다

n. **major**
v. **to major in**

전공이 뭐예요? What is your major?
저는 대학에서 경제학을 **전공하고** 있습니다.
At college, I am majoring in economics.

18 지내다

v. **to spend (one's) time; to get along**

그동안 어떻게 **지내셨어요**? How have you been?
소현이는 새 룸메이트하고 잘 **지내요**.
Sohyeon gets along well with her new roommate.

syn. 보내다 *v.* to pass, spend time → 5-9

19 칼

n. **knife, sword**

아이들이 장난감 **칼**을 가지고 놀고 있어요.
Children are playing with toy swords.
이 **칼**은 야채를 자를 때 쓰세요.
Use this knife is for cutting vegetables.

20 화장실(化粧室)

n. **restroom**

공중 화장실 public restroom
손이 좀 더러워졌네요. 실례지만, **화장실**이 어디예요?
My hands got a little dirty. Excuse me, but where is the restroom?

CHECK UP

결혼, 기숙사, 무척, 방금, 선택, 약, 일기예보, 전공, 칼, 화장실

1 choice ....

2 dormitory ....

3 just now ....

4 knife, sword ....

5 major ....

6 marriage ....

7 medicine ....

8 restroom ....

9 very, really, extremely ....

10 weather forecast ....

CHECK UP

다니다, 덥다, 따뜻하다, 맑다, 부지런하다, 사용하다, 쉽다,
심하다, 외출하다, 지내다

1 to be clear ____________

2 to be diligent, hard working ____________

3 to be easy ____________

4 to be serious, severe, harsh ____________

5 to be hot ____________

6 to be warm ____________

7 to go out ____________

8 to go (and attend) regularly ____________

9 to spend time, get along ____________

10 to use ____________

Circle the correct spelling 1

1	AIRPLANE	□ 피행기	□ 비행기		
2	BED	□ 침대	□ 짐대	□ 침데	□ 짐데
3	BOOK	□ 책	□ 첵		
4	BUILDING	□ 빌딩	□ 필딩		
5	CHINA	□ 중국	□ 종국	□ 충국	
6	COFFEE SHOP	□ 커피숍	□ 커피숖	□ 커피숍	□ 커피셥
7	COMPANY	□ 회사	□ 희사		
8	DAD	□ 아바	□ 압바	□ 아빠	□ 어삐
9	DEPARTMENT STORE	□ 백화점	□ 백화전		
10	DINNER	□ 저녁	□ 저년		
11	FAMILY	□ 가족	□ 가죽	□ 가속	
12	FOR THE FIRST TIME	□ 처음	□ 초음	□ 저음	
13	FRIEND	□ 친구	□ 진구	□ 친국	
14	GRADUATION	□ 졸업	□ 절업	□ 촐업	
15	HELLO	□ 안녕하세요?	□ 안영하세요?		
16	HIGH SCHOOL	□ 고든학생	□ 고등학생		
17	HOMEWORK	□ 숙제	□ 죽제	□ 속제	
18	HOUSE	□ 집	□ 십	□ 깁	
19	I	□ 저	□ 처		
20	JAPAN	□ 일본	□ 일번		
21	KOREA	□ 한국	□ 학국		
22	MAJOR	□ 전공	□ 정공	□ 천공	□ 존공
23	MOM	□ 엄아	□ 엄마	□ 어마	
24	MONDAY	□ 월요일	□ 왈요일		
25	PARENTS	□ 부모님	□ 보무님	□ 부무님	

Answer

1 비행기 2 침대 3 책 4 빌딩 5 중국 6 커피숍 7 회사 8 아빠 9 백화점 10 저녁 11 가족 12 처음 13 친구 14 졸업 15 안녕하세요? 16 고등학생 17 숙제 18 집 19 저 20 일본 21 한국 22 전공 23 엄마 24 월요일 25 부모님

LESSON 17

1 **경제(經濟)** *n.* **economy**

경제학 economics

요즘 세계 **경제**가 안 좋아요.
The global economy is not good these days.

오늘 **경제학** 시험이 있어요. I have an economics test today.

2 **기차(汽車)** *n.* **train** ⋯▸Appendix I

기차를 타다 to ride in a train, 기차역 train station

서울에 가는 **기차** 요금이 얼마예요?
How much is the railroad fare to Seoul?

할머니 집까지 **기차**로 4시간 걸려요.
It takes four hours to my grandma's house by train.

3 **다르다** *adj.* **to be different**

(르) 달라–다릅니다–다를–다른

소현이와 소피아는 친구예요. 그런데 성격이 아주 **달라요**.
Sohyeon and Sophia are friends. However, their personalities are very different.

오늘은 **다른** 음식을 먹을까요?
Do you want to try different food today?

ant. (똑)같다 *adj.* **to be (exactly) same** ⋯▸9-1

4 **덮다** *v.* **to cover**

이불을 잘 **덮고** 주무세요. Sleep with your blankets tucked in well.

아직 수업이 안 끝났으니까 교과서를 **덮지** 마세요.
Because the class is not over yet, don't close your textbooks.

5 **따르다** *v.* **to follow**

(르) 따라–따릅니다–따를–따르는

저는 엄마를 **따라서** 백화점에 갔어요.
I tagged along with my mother to the department store.

This word is generally used in such compound verbs as 따라가다 'to follow; to go after', 따라오다 'to follow; to come with', and 따라하다 'to repeat after; to imitate what the other person does'.

이 길을 **따라가면** 서울로 갈 수 있어요.
If you follow this road, you can get to Seoul.

저를 **따라오세요**. Please follow me.

한국어를 잘 하고 싶으면 한국 사람 발음을 많이 **따라** 하세요.
If you want to speak Korean well, repeat (imitate) Korean people's pronunciation a lot.

6 **맞다** — *v.* **to be correct, right; to fit, suit**

어느 답이 **맞아요**? Which answer is correct?

옷이 잘 **맞아요**? Do these clothes fit you well?

ant. 틀리다 *v.* to be incorrect, wrong

7 **문제(問題)** — *n.* **question, problem**

수학 문제 math problem, 문제를 풀다 to solve a question

첫 번째 **문제**의 답은 3번이에요.
The answer to the first question is number 3.

자동차에 **문제**가 생겼어요. My car has got a problem.

8 **방법(方法)** — *n.* **way, means, method**

한국어를 잘하는 **방법**을 알고 싶어요.
I want to know a method to speak Korean well.

9 **부치다** — *v.* **to send (a letter or money)**

편지를 부치다 to send a letter, 돈을 부치다 to remit (send) money

저는 소포를 **부치러** 우체국에 가고 있어요.
I am going to the post office to send a package.

엄마가 학비를 **부쳐** 주셨어요. Mother sent me the tuition.

Be careful not to confuse this word with 붙이다 'to attach' → 25-9

syn. 보내다 *v.* to send → 5-9

10 **사이** — *n.* **gap or space (between); (personal) relationship**

은행은 식당하고 우체국 **사이**에 있어요.
The bank is between the restaurant and the post office.

저는 남동생하고 **사이**가 좋아요.
I get along well with my younger brother.

11 설거지 *n.* dishwashing
설거지하다 *v.* to wash dishes

엄마는 요리를 하시고, 아빠는 **설거지**를 하세요.
My mom cooks and my dad washes the dishes.

Be careful not to spell as "설겆이", which is a common mistake, even among Korean people.

rel. 집안일 *n.* household chores

12 슬프다 *adj.* to be sad

(ㅡ) 슬퍼 – 슬픕니다 – 슬플 – 슬픈

지난 주에 할머니가 돌아가셨어요. 정말 **슬퍼요**.
I am really sad because my grandmother passed away last week.
저는 **슬픈** 영화를 좋아해요. I like sad movies.

ant. 기쁘다 *adj.* to be glad, happy, 즐겁다 *adj.* to be pleasant, to be joyful ⋯13-18.

13 싱겁다 *adj.* to be bland

(ㅂ) 싱거워 – 싱겁습니다 – 싱거울 – 싱거운

엄마, 국이 좀 **싱거워요**. 소금 좀 주세요.
Mom, the soup tastes a little bland. Please pass me the salt.

rel. 짜다 *adj.* to be salty; 맵다 *adj.* to be spicy, hot ⋯20-6

14 약속(約束) [약쏙] *n.* promise
약속하다 [약쏘카다] *v.* to make a promise

약속을 지키다 to keep one's promise
나는 내가 한 **약속**은 꼭 **지켜요**.
I always keep the promises that I make.
내일 꼭 오세요. **약속해** 주세요.
You must come tomorrow. Promise me.

15 요금(料金) *n.* fee, fare

택시를 타면 빨리 갈 수 있지만 **요금**이 비싸요.
If you take a taxi, you can go faster, but the taxi fare is expensive.

The first character 요 is written 료 if it is not the first syllable in the word, and it compounds many words such as 전기료 'electricity bill', 수업료 'tuition', or 통신료 'communication costs'.

16 일어나다

v. **to get up**

오늘은 시험이 있어서 아침 6시에 **일어났어요**.
Because I have an exam today, I got up at 6 in the morning.

rel. 깨다 *v.* to wake (up)

17 전화(電話)

n. **phone call, telephone**

전화하다 to make a call (= 전화를 걸다), 전화번호 telephone number, 전화비 telephone bill, 전화기 telephone (set), 휴대전화 cell phone (= 핸드폰, 휴대폰)

저는 거의 매일 집에 **전화**를 **해요**. I call home almost every day.

요즘 사람들은 거의 하루 종일 **전화기**를 쓴다.
People these days use their phones almost all day long.

rel. 스마트폰 *n.* smart phone

18 지다

v. **to be defeated; to lose**

우리 팀이 상대 팀에게 1 대 2로 **졌다**.
My team lost the game to the opposite team by two to one.

ant. 이기다 *v.* to win →8-16

19 크다

(—) 커 - 큽니다 - 클 - 큰

adj. **to be big**

크기 size

어제 산 셔츠가 나한테 너무 **커요**.
The shirt that I bought yesterday is too large for me.

저는 **큰** 도시에서 살고 싶어요. I want to live in a big city.

ant. 작다 *adj.* to be small →6-17

20 회사(會社)

n. **company**

회사원 company employee, worker

우리 언니는 뉴욕에 있는 **회사**에 다녀요.
My older sister works for a company in New York.

CHECK UP

경제, 기차, 문제, 방법, 사이, 설거지, 약속, 요금, 전화, 회사

1 company ____________

2 dishwashing ____________

3 economy ____________

4 fee, fare ____________

5 gap, space, relationship ____________

6 promise ____________

7 question, problem ____________

8 telephone, phone call, ____________

9 train ____________

10 way, method ____________

CHECK UP

다르다, 덮다, 따르다, 맞다, 부치다, 슬프다, 싱겁다, 일어나다, 지다, 크다

1 to be big ______

2 to be correct; to fit ______

3 to be defeated, lose ______

4 to be different ______

5 to be sad ______

6 to cover ______

7 to follow ______

8 to get up ______

9 to send (a letter, money) ______

10 to be bland ______

Circle the correct spelling 2

1	MY (humble)	□ 제	□ 재		
2	MY (plain)	□ 내	□ 네		
3	NAME	□ 이름	□ 일음	□ 일름	
4	OLDER BROTHER	□ 오빠	□ 어빠		
5	OUTSIDE	□ 밖	□ 빢	□ 빡	
6	PIG	□ 돼지	□ 되지	□ 뒤지	
7	PRESENT	□ 선물	□ 성물		
8	QUESTION	□ 질문	□ 칠문		
9	SCHOOL YEAR	□ 학년	□ 한년		
10	STUDENT	□ 학생	□ 핵생		
11	THURSDAY	□ 먹요일	□ 목요일		
12	TO BE MANY	□ 마나요	□ 만나요	□ 만아요	□ 많아요
13	TO LIKE	□ 좋아하다	□ 촣아하다		
14	TODAY	□ 오늘	□ 오널	□ 오눌	
15	TOMORROW	□ 네일	□ 내일		
16	TRIP	□ 여행	□ 영행		
17	TWENTY YEARS OLD	□ 수무살	□ 스무살	□ 스물살	
18	WASHING DISHES	□ 설거지	□ 설겂이		
19	WELL	□ 잘	□ 찰		
20	WHAT DAY?	□ 며칠	□ 몇일	□ 몇칠	
21	WHAT KIND OF	□ 무슨	□ 무순		
22	WHAT NUMBER?	□ 몇	□ 멷		
23	WHAT	□ 뭐	□ 뫄		
24	YESTERDAY	□ 어제	□ 어재		
25	YOUNGER SISTER	□ 영동생	□ 여동생	□ 여덩생	

Answer

1 제 2 내 3 이름 4 오빠 5 밖 6 돼지 7 선물 8 질문 9 학년 10 학생 11 목요일 12 많아요 13 좋아하다 14 오늘 15 내일 16 여행 17 스무살 18 설거지 19 잘 20 며칠 21 무슨 22 몇 23 뭐 24 어제 25 여동생

LESSON 18

1 **경찰(警察)** *n.* **the police; policeman**

경찰관 police man, 경찰서 police station, 교통 경찰 traffic police

경찰이 도둑을 잡았어요. The police caught the thief/robber.

집에 도둑이 들어서 **경찰**에 신고를 했어요.
My house was robbed last night, so I reported it to the police.

2 **길다** *adj.* **to be long**

(ㄹ) 길어 – 깁니다 – 길 – 긴

저는 머리가 **길어요**. My hair is long.

한국에서는 여름 방학이 짧고 겨울 방학이 **길어요**.
In Korea, summer vacation is short and winter vacation is long.

긴 겨울이 끝나고 봄이 됐어요.
After a long winter, spring has come.

ant. 짧다 *adj.* **to be short** 23-18

3 **다리** *n.* **bridge**

맨해튼에서 **다리**를 지나면 뉴저지예요.
If you go across the bridge from Manhattan, you'll be in New Jersey.

In Korea, many large bridges are called 대교, e.g., 한강 대교 'Hangang Bridge', 마포 대교 'Mapo Bridge'.

rel. 다리 *n.* **leg (homonym)**

4 **도로(道路)** *n.* **road, street**

고속도로 highway, freeway

교통사고로 **도로**가 막혔어요.
Because of an accident, the road is blocked.

syn. 길 *n.* **street, road**

5 **따로** *adv.* **separately; additionally**

저는 예전에는 부모님하고 같이 살았는데 지금은 **따로** 살아요.
I used to live with my parents, but now I live separately from them.

ant. 같이 *adv.* **together** 10-1

6 **매우** — *adv.* **very much, extremely**

그 문제는 **매우** 어려웠습니다. The question was very hard.

매우 is usually used in more formal or written texts compared to other synnomyms.

syn. 굉장히 →2-2, 대단히 *adv.* **very much** →7-4; 아주 →6-14

7 **문화(文化)** — *n.* **culture**

요즘 전 세계의 많은 사람들이 한국 대중 **문화**에 관심이 많아요.
These days, many people around the world are interested in Korean pop culture.

8 **방송(放送)** — *n.* **broadcasting**
방송하다 — *v.* **to broadcast**

방송되다 *v.* to be broadcast

방송국 broadcasting station

요즘은 전화기로도 TV **방송**을 볼 수 있어요.
These days you can also watch TV broadcasting programs on your phones.

9 **부탁(付託)** — *n.* **favor, request**
부탁하다 [부타카다] — *v.* **to ask a favor**

부탁을 들어주다 to do somebody a favor

아버지, 제 **부탁** 좀 **들어주세요**. Father, please do me a favor.

잘 **부탁**드립니다. I wish for your kind help.
(This is a conventional formulaic expression people exchange when they meet for the first time.)

10 **사장(社長)** — *n.* **president of a company, CEO**

저희 회사 **사장님**은 아침에 제일 먼저 출근하세요.
The CEO of our company comes to work the earliest in the morning.

When 사장 is used as an address term, honorific suffix －님 is often attached as in 사장님. Further, 사장님 is often used as a general address term for a middle aged man who is not actually a president.

11 **설명하다(說明–)** *v.* **to explain**
설명 *n.* **explanation**

선생님, 왜 2번이 답이에요? 좀 설명해 주세요.
Teacher, why is No. 2 the correct answer? Please explain it to me.
아주 쉬워요. 제 설명을 잘 들어 보세요.
It's really easy. Listen to my explantion carefully.

12 **습관(習慣) [습꽌]** *n.* **habit**

저는 글씨는 오른손으로 쓰고, 마우스는 왼손으로 해요. 습관이에요.
I write with my right hand and use the mouse with my left hand. It's my habit.
현우는 일찍 일어나는 좋은 습관이 있어요.
Hyeonwu has a good habit of getting up early in the morning.

syn. 버릇 *n.* **(bad) habit**

13 **싸다** *adj.* **to be cheap**

가: 셔츠가 아주 좋은 것 같아요. Your shirt looks very nice.
나: 아니에요. 그냥 싼 거예요. No. It's just a cheap one.

ant. 비싸다 *adj.* **to be expensive** → 3-10

14 **어렵다** *adj.* **to be difficult, hard**

(ㅂ) 어려워 – 어렵습니다 – 어려울 – 어려운

이 선생님, 시험이 너무 어려워요.
Professor Lee, the exam is too hard.
어려운 문제가 너무 많아요. There are too many difficult problems.

ant. 쉽다 *adj.* **to be easy** → 16-12

15 **요리(料理)** *n.* **cooking** → Appendix E
요리하다 *v.* **to cook**

요리사 chef, cook
저는 집에서 한국 요리를 자주 해요.
I often cook Korean food at home.
제 취미는 요리하는 것이에요. My hobby is cooking.

16 일찍

adv. **early**

어젯밤에는 너무 피곤해서 일찍 잤어요.
I was too tired last night, so I went to bed early.
수업에 일찍 오세요. Please come to class early.

ant. 늦게 *adv.* **late** ⋯ 15-3; *rel.* 빨리 *adv.* **quickly** ⋯ 6-10

17 점수(點數) [점쑤]

n. **score, point**

오늘 게임을 했는데 제가 가장 높은 점수를 받았어요.
I played a game today and received the highest score.
제 시험 점수가 어때요? How is my test score?

rel. 학점 *n.* **credit, grade**; 성적 *n.* **grade.**

18 지도(地圖)

n. **map**

세계 지도 world map
지도가 없어서 길을 잃었어요. Because I don't have a map, I am lost.

rel. 약도 *n.* **rough map (for a direction)**

19 키

n. **height**

키가 크다 to be tall, 키가 작다 to be short
이제 내가 아빠보다 키가 더 커요. I am taller than my dad now.

The word 키 generally refers to the height of people. Note that 길다 'to be long' and 짧다 'to be short' are not used for describing one's height in Korean.
The height of a building should be said to be high (건물이 높다) or low (건물이 낮다).

20 회의(會議)
[회의 or 훼이]
회의하다

n. **meeting, conference**

v. **to have a meeting**

회의실 meeting room
생물학 수업 그룹 프로젝트 때문에 오늘 저녁에 회의가 있어요.
For the group project in Biology class, I'm going to have a meeting tonight.

CHECK UP

경찰, 다리, 도로, 문화, 사장, 습관, 요리, 점수, 지도, 키

1 bridge ______

2 president of a company, CEO ______

3 cooking ______

4 culture ______

5 habit ______

6 height ______

7 map ______

8 police, policeman ______

9 road, street ______

10 score, point ______

CHECK UP

길다, 따로, 매우, 방송하다, 부탁하다, 설명하다, 싸다,
어렵다, 일찍, 회의하다

1 early ____________________

2 separately, additionally ____________________

3 to ask a favor ____________________

4 to be cheap ____________________

5 to be difficult, hard ____________________

6 to be long ____________________

7 to broadcast ____________________

8 to explain ____________________

9 to have a meeting ____________________

10 very much, extremely ____________________

과목과 전공 Subjects and Majors

간호학 Nursing Science

건축학 Architecture

경영학 Business Administration

경제학 Economics

교육학 Education

국제학 International Studies

기계공학 Mechanical Engineering

동아시아학 East Asian Studies

문학 Literature

물리학 Physics

미술 Art

법학 Law

비교문학 Comparative Literature

사학 History

사회복지학 Social Work Studies

생물학 Biology

생화학 Bio Chemistry

수학 Mathematics

신문방송학 Communication Studies

심리학 Psychology

약학 Pharmacy

언어학 Linguistics

음악 Music

의학 Medical Science

전자공학 Electrical Engineering

정치학 Political Science

컴퓨터공학 Computer Engineering

한국학 Korean Studies

화학 Chemistry

회계학 Accounting

LESSON 19

1 **계시다** *adj.* **to exist; to be at (honorific)**

저는 한국에 있어요. 그런데 아버지는 미국에 **계세요**.
I am in Korea, but my father is in America.

This word is the honorific form of 있다. ⋯▸24-15 While 있다 has the meanings of both "existence" and "possession" as in 저는 지금 도서관에 있어요. 'I am in the library now.' and 저는 숙제가 있어요. 'I have homework', "계시다" does not have the meaning of "possession". For that purpose, "있으시다" should be used.

선생님, 오늘 오후에 시간이 있으세요? (계세요 is ungrammatical here)
Teacher, do you have time this afternoon?

2 **깨끗하다 [깨끄타다]** *adj.* **to be clean**

이 아파트는 싸고 **깨끗해요**.
This apartment is cheap and clean.
조용하고 **깨끗한** 방 있어요?
Do you have a quiet and clean room?

ant. 더럽다 *adj.* to be dirty ⋯▸13-4

3 **다시** *adv.* **again, once more**

다시 한 번 말씀해 주세요. Please say it once again.
우리 **다시**는 만나지 마요. Let's not meet ever again.

4 **도서관 (圖書館)** *n.* **library**

도서관에서 책을 빌리려고 해요.
I am intending to borrow a book from the library.

5 **땀** *n.* **sweat**

땀이 나다 to sweat, 땀을 흘리다 to sweat, perspire.
오늘은 날씨가 더워서 10분 걸었는데 **땀**이 많이 **나네요**.
Since the weather is hot today, after walking for 10 minutes I started to sweat a lot.
찜질방에서 **땀**을 좀 **흘리고** 나면 기분이 좋아요.
It feels good after sweating a little at a *jjimjilbang* (Korean style dry sauna).

6 **매일(每日)** *n./adv.* **every day**

저는 **매일** 두 시간씩 한국어를 공부합니다.
I study Korean for two hours every day.

매 means 'each' or 'every' and combines with most time words: 매시간 every hour, 매주 every week, 매년 every year, 매달 or 매월 every month, 매번 every time, 매 학기 every semester

syn. 날마다 *adv.* every day

7 **묻다** *v.* **to ask**

(ㄷ) 물어 – 묻습니다 – 물을 – 묻는

물어보다 to inquire

말씀 좀 **묻겠습니다**. Let me ask you something.

모르는 게 있으면 저한테 **물어보세요**.
If there is anything you don't know, please ask me.

rel. 대답하다 *v.* to answer ⋯ 5-4

8 **방학(放學)** *n.* **school vacation, break**

여름/겨울 방학 summer/winter vacation

저는 이번 **여름 방학**에 한국에 여행 갈 거예요.
I will go on a trip to Korea this summer break.

For a general word for vacation or break other than students' vacations is 휴가 as used in 휴가를 가다 'to go on a vacation'.

9 **분위기(雰圍氣)** *n.* **atmosphere, ambience, mood, air**

이 커피숍은 **분위기**가 좋아요.
The atmosphere of this coffee shop is great.

그 장례식의 **분위기**는 아주 슬펐습니다.
The atmosphere at the funeral was very sad.

10 **사전(辭典)** *n.* **dictionary**

한영 사전 Korean-English dictionary

전자 사전 electronic dictionary

이 단어를 **사전**에서 찾아보세요.
Look up this word in the dictionary.

11 **성(姓)** *n.* **family name**

노아 씨, **성**이 어떻게 되세요? Noah, what is your last name?

한국에서는 결혼한 후에 여자가 남편의 **성**을 쓰지 않아요.
In Korea, women don't use to their husband's last name after they get married.

rel. 이름 *n.* **(first) name**, 성함 *n.* **(full) name (honorific)**

12 **시간(時間)** *n.* **time; hours (counter for duration)**

오늘 밤에 **시간** 있어요? Do you have time tonight?

한국까지 비행기로 열 **시간**쯤 걸렸어요.
It took me about 10 hours to Korea by airplane.

Note that 시간 is to express duration of time as in 한 시간 'one hour', 두 시간 'two hours', 세 시간 'three hours', while 시 means point of time as in 한 시 'one o'clock', 두 시 'two o'clock', and 세 시 'three o'clock'.

13 **싸우다** *v.* **to fight, argue**

저는 제 언니가 정말 좋아요. 그런데 어릴 때는 자주 **싸웠어요**.
I like my sister very much. But we often argued when I was younger.

14 **어리다** *adj.* **to be young**

어린이 *n.* child

제 여동생은 저보다 두 살 **어립니다**.
My younger sister is two years younger than I am.

저는 **어렸을** 때 부산에서 살았어요.
When I was young, I used to live in Busan.

ant. 나이가 많다 *adj.* **to be old**

15 **요즘** *n.* **these days, nowadays**

저는 시험 때문에 **요즘** 잠을 잘 못 자요.
I cannot sleep well these days because of exams.

요즘 어떻게 지내세요? How are you these days?

syn. 요새 *adv.* **these days**

16 읽다 [익따] *v.* to read (something)

제 남동생은 일주일에 책을 두 권쯤 읽어요.
My younger brother reads about two books a week.

Note that it sounds unnatural if you don't specify any object for 읽다 as in "저는 읽어요". If you don't want to give the specific information about what you read, you can say something like 저는 뭐 좀 읽어요. 'I just read something.'

17 점심(點心) *n.* lunch

점심 시간 lunch time
월요일에는 수업이 많아서 점심을 못 먹어요.
I have many classes on Monday, so I can't eat lunch.

rel. 아침 **morning/breakfast**, 저녁 **evening/dinner**

18 지하철(地下鐵) *n.* subway

지하철역 subway station
서울에서는 버스보다 지하철로 가는 것이 더 빨라요.
It is faster to go by subway than by bus in Seoul.

rel. 지하 **underground, below**, 지하실 **basement**, 지하도 **underpass**

19 타다 *v.* to get in (on); to ride

시간이 별로 없으니까 우리 택시를 탈까요?
Because we don't have much time, should we take a taxi?
이 길에서는 자전거를 타면 위험해요.
It is dangerous to ride a bicycle on this road.

타고 다니다 and 타고 가다 means 'to travel by (a means of transportation).
저는 학교에 버스를 **타고** 다녀요. I go to school by bus.
수업 시간에 늦어서 학교까지 택시를 **타고** 갔어요.
Because I was late for school, I went to school by taxi.

rel. 내리다 *v.* **to get off (from a transportation)**

20 횡단보도(橫斷步道) *n.* crosswalk →Appendix F

길을 건널 때는 횡단보도로 건너야 해요.
When you cross the street, you must cross at a crosswalk.

CHECK UP

도서관, 땀, 방학, 분위기, 사전, 성, 시간, 점심, 지하철, 횡단보도

1 atmosphere, mood ______

2 crosswalk ______

3 dictionary ______

4 family name ______

5 library ______

6 lunch ______

7 school vacation, break ______

8 subway ______

9 sweat ______

10 time ______

CHECK UP

계시다, 깨끗하다, 다시, 매일, 묻다, 싸우다, 어리다, 요즘, 읽다, 타다

1 again ....

2 every day ....

3 these days ....

4 to ask ....

5 to be clean ....

6 to be young ....

7 to exist, to be at (honorific) ....

8 to fight ....

9 to read ....

10 to ride, get in ....

단과대학 Schools/Colleges at a University

간호대학(간호대) School of Nursing

경영대학(경영대) School of Business

공과대학(공대) School of Engineering

문과대학(문대) School of Liberal Arts

문리대학(문리대) School of Arts and Sciences

미술대학(미대) School of Art

법과대학(법대) School of Law

사범대학(사대) School of Education

약학대학(약대) School of Pharmacy

음악대학(음대) School of Music

의과대학(의대) School of Medicine

이과대학(이과대) School of Natural Sciences

치과대학(치대) School of Dentistry

LESSON 20

1 **계절 (季節)** *n.* **season (of a year)**

사계절 four seasons

제가 좋아하는 **계절**은 봄이에요. My favorite season is spring.

한국에는 **사계절**이 있어요. There are four seasons in Korea.

rel. 봄 *n.* **spring**, 여름 *n.* **summer**, 가을 *n.* **fall**, 겨울 *n.* **winter**

2 **꽃 [꼳]** *n.* **flower**

꽃집 flower shop, 꽃이 피다 to bloom, 꽃이 지다 to wither

한국에서 봄에 피는 **꽃**에는 진달래와 개나리가 있어요.
In Korea, the flowers blooming in spring are azaleas and forsythias.

3 **다음** *n.* **next, following**

다음 주 next week, 다음 달 next month, 다음 해 next year

다음 사람 들어오세요. Next person, please come in.

저는 **다음** 학기에도 계속 한국어 수업을 들을 거예요.
Next semester, I will continue taking a Korean class.

~(은)ㄴ 다음에 after ~ing

수업 끝난 다음에 어디에 갈 거예요? After finishing the class, where are you going?

ant. 지난 **last, past (event)** ⋯ 15-18

4 **도시(都市)** *n.* **city**

대도시 large city, 중소도시 mid-sized and small cities

한국에서 제일 큰 **도시**는 서울이에요.
The biggest city in Korea is Seoul.

저는 큰 **도시**보다 시골에서 살고 싶어요.
Rather than in a big city, I want to live in the countryside.

rel. 수도 *n.* **capital city (of a country)** ⋯ 9-12

5 **떠나다** *v.* **to leave**

~을 떠나다 to leave ~ ~(으)로 떠나다 to leave for ~

지하철이 방금 **떠났어요**. The subway train just left.

저는 내일 서울로 **떠나요**.
I leave for Seoul tomorrow.
저는 내일 서울을 **떠나요**.
I leave Seoul tomorrow.

6 **맵다** — *adj.* **to taste spicy, hot**

(ㅂ) 매워 – 맵습니다 – 매울 – 매운

이 고추장은 너무 **매워요**.
This red pepper paste is too hot.
한국 음식들 중에는 **매운** 음식이 많아요.
In Korean cuisine, there are many spicy foods.

rel. 짜다 *adj.* **to be salty**, 달다 *adj.* **to be sweet** → 24-3, 쓰다 *adj.* **to be bitter**, 시다 *adj.* **to be sour**, 싱겁다 *adj.* **to be bland** → 17-3

7 **물건(物件)** — *n.* **thing; item; product**

이 가게에서는 여러 가지 **물건**들을 팔고 있어요.
This store sells various kinds of items.

8 **배달(配達)** — *n.* **delivery**
배달하다 — *v.* **to deliver**

우편 배달 mail delivery, 배달시키다 to ask for delivery
한국에서는 햄버거도 **배달해** 줘요.
They even deliver hamburgers in Korea.

9 **불다** — *v.* **to blow; to play (wind instruments)**

(ㄹ) 불어 – 붑니다 – 불 – 부는

오늘은 바람이 많이 **붑니다**.
It is very windy today.
저는 취미로 플루트를 **불어요**.
I play flute as a hobby.

10 **사진 (寫眞)** — *n.* **picture, photograph**

사진을 찍다 to take a picture
가족 **사진**이 정말 잘 나왔어요.
Your family picture looks wonderful. (*lit.*, Your family picture came out really well.)

11 성격(性格) [성껵] *n.* **personality**

성격이 좋다/나쁘다 to have a good/bad personality

성격이 다른 사람하고 결혼하는 것이 좋을까요, 안 좋을까요?

Do you think it is good or bad to marry someone with a different personality?

12 시골 *n.* **the countryside, rural area**

저는 도시에서만 살아서 **시골**로 여행가는 걸 좋아해요.

Because I have only lived in the city, I like to take trips to the countryside.

ant. 도시 *n.* **city** →20-4

13 쌓이다 [싸이다] *v.* **to get stacked, increase**

스트레스가 **쌓이면** 어떻게 푸세요?

When you're stressed, how do you relieve it?

눈이 많이 **쌓였어요**. The snow has piled up a lot.

~을/를 쌓다 to stack (something)

책을 여기에 **쌓으세요**. Please stack the books here.

14 어른 *n.* **adult, (one's) elders**

네가 대학생이면 이제 **어른**이다.

If you are a college student, you are an adult now.

ant. 어린이 **child** →19-14, 아이 **child** →5-14

15 우산(雨傘) *n.* **umbrella**

우산을 쓰다 to put on an umbrella

지금 밖에 비가 와요. **우산** 가지고 왔어요?

It's raining outside now. Did you bring your umbrella?

우산 없으시면 이거 쓰세요.

If you don't have an umbrella, please use this.

16 잃다 [일타] | *v.* **to lose**

돈을 잃다 to lose money (in gambling or stock markets), 길을 잃다 to get lost (*lit.*, to lose the road)

지난번에 운전면허 시험에 떨어져서 자신감을 **잃었어요**.
Since I failed the last drivers' license test, I lost my confidence.

In speech, 잃어버리다 is more frequently used than 잃다. e.g. 어제 운전면허증을 **잃어버렸어요**. Yesterday, I lost my driver's license.

Make sure not to be confused with 잊어버리다 'to forget (completely)'.

17 정류장(停留場) [정뉴장] | *n.* **(bus) stop**

버스 정류장 bus stop

다음 **정류장**이 어디예요? What is the next stop?

rel. 지하철역 *n.* **subway station** ⋯→19-18, 기차역 *n.* **train station** ⋯→25-14

18 직업(職業) [지겁] | *n.* **occupation, career, job**

나는 나한테 제일 잘 맞는 전공과 **직업**을 고르고 싶다.
I want to choose a major and an occupation that are right for me.

rel. 직장 *n.* **workplace**

19 태어나다 | *v.* **to be born**

제가 세 살 때 제 남동생이 **태어났어요**.
My younger brother was born when I was three.

저는 서울에서 **태어나서** 자랐어요. I was born and raised in Seoul.

rel. 자라다 *v.* **to grow, to be raised** ⋯→3-17

20 휴대전화(携帶電話) | *n.* **mobile phone, cell phone** ⋯→17-17

오늘 지갑하고 **휴대전화**를 집에 두고 나왔어요.
I left my wallet and cell phone at home today.

syn. 휴대폰, 핸드폰 *n.* **cell phone**

CHECK UP

계절, 꽃, 도시, 물건, 사진, 시골, 어른, 우산, 정류장, 직업, 휴대전화

1 (bus) stop ______________

2 adult ______________

3 city ______________

4 countryside, rural area ______________

5 flower ______________

6 mobile phone, cell phone ______________

7 occupation, job ______________

8 picture, photograph ______________

9 season ______________

10 thing, item ______________

11 umbrella ______________

CHECK UP

다음, 떠나다, 맵다, 배달하다, 불다, 성격, 쌓이다, 잃다, 태어나다

1 next ____________

2 personality ____________

3 to be born ____________

4 to blow, play wind instruments ____________

5 to deliver ____________

6 to get stacked, increase ____________

7 to leave ____________

8 to lose ____________

9 to taste spicy, hot ____________

REVIEW Exercises

Choose the one which is most appropriate in the blank.

1 저는 내년에 여자 친구__________ 결혼할 거예요.

① 를 ② 하고 ③ 가 ④ 한테

2 제 동생은 고등학생인데 내년부터 대학교에 __________.

① 다닐 거예요 ② 들을 거예요 ③ 볼 거예요 ④ 배울 거예요

3 감기에 걸려서 약을 __________ 잤어요.

① 가지고 ② 마시고 ③ 먹고 ④ 하고

4 오래간만이네요. 그동안 어떻게 __________?

① 왔어요 ② 보내요 ③ 살아요 ④ 지냈어요

5 현우는 키가 __________. 그래도 농구를 잘 해요.

① 작아요 ② 짧아요 ③ 길어요 ④ 낮아요

6 오늘 방을 청소했어요. 그래서 방이 아주 __________

① 넓어요 ② 좁아요 ③ 더러워요 ④ 깨끗해요

7 수업 시간에 늦어서 학교까지 택시를 __________ 갔어요.

① 타면서 ② 타다가 ③ 타고 ④ 타러

8 제가 제일 좋아하는 __________은 봄이에요.

① 계절 ② 달 ③ 시간 ④ 월

9 오늘은 춥고 바람이 많이 __________.

① 나요 ② 불어요 ③ 날려요 ④ 불러요

10 저는 비싼 시계를 ________________. 아무리 찾아도 못 찾겠어요.

① 잊어버렸어요 ② 잊었어요 ③ 잃어버렸어요 ④ 없어졌어요

11 저는 서울에서 __________ 자랐어요.

① 다녀서 ② 태어나서 ③ 커서 ④ 나와서

12 이 커피는 너무 __________ 조금 이따가 마실 거예요.

① 더워서 ② 매워서 ③ 뜨거워서 ④ 추워서

13 이 방은 좀 __________. 에어컨을 틀어 주세요.

① 뜨거워요 ② 더워요 ③ 따뜻해요 ④ 시원해요

14 비가 오네요. 우산을 같이 __________.

① 써요 ② 들어요 ③ 입어요 ④ 신어요

15 봄이 되어서 공원에 꽃이 많이 __________.

① 피었어요 ② 나왔어요 ③ 시들었어요 ④ 피워요

Choose the one that can replace the underlined part.

16 어제는 <u>무척</u> 더운 날이었어요.

① 매우 ② 좀 ③ 금방 ④ 금방

17 저는 <u>매일</u> 두 시간씩 한국어를 공부해요.

① 매주 ② 하루종일 ③ 날마다 ④ 가끔

18 지하철이 <u>방금</u> 떠났어요.

① 곧 ② 금방 ③ 조금 ④ 후에

REVIEW Exercises

19 2층 화장실은 오늘 쓰지 마세요.

① 보지 ② 들어가지 ③ 열지 ④ 사용하지

20 저는 소포를 부치러 우체국에 갔어요.

① 보내러 ② 붙이러 ③ 사러 ④ 붙어서

Choose the one that has the opposite meaning to the underlined part.

21 이 호수는 물이 맑아요.

① 깨끗해요 ② 흐려요 ③ 구름이 끼었어요 ④ 햇빛이 나요

22 이 음식이 너무 짜서 못 먹겠어요.

① 싱거워서 ② 맛있어서 ③ 맛없어서 ④ 달아서

23 한국 팀이 축구 경기에서 이겼어요.

① 잃었어요 ② 졌어요 ③ 놀았어요 ④ 찼어요

24 네가 대학생이면 이제 어른이다.

① 학생 ② 아기 ③ 노인 ④ 어린이

25 어제 우산을 잃어버렸어요.

① 잊어버렸어요 ② 잊었어요 ③ 찾았어요 ④ 이겼어요

Answer

1 ② 2 ① 3 ③ 4 ④ 5 ① 6 ④ 7 ③ 8 ① 9 ② 10 ③ 11 ② 12 ③ 13 ② 14 ①
15 ① 16 ① 17 ③ 18 ② 19 ④ 20 ① 21 ② 22 ① 23 ② 24 ④ 25 ③

LESSON 21

1 **계획(計劃)** *n.* **plan**
계획하다 [계획카다] *v.* **to plan**

계획을 세우다 to make plans, 계획을 짜다 to make/lay out a plan

이번 주말에 무슨 **계획**이 있으세요?
Do you have any plans this weekend?

계획을 너무 많이 세우면 지킬 수가 없잖아요.
If you make too many plans, you cannot keep all of them.

계획을 만들다 makes sense, but 계획을 세우다 is a more commonly used phrase.

2 **꿈** *n.* **dream**

꿈을 꾸다 to dream

좋은 **꿈 꾸세요**! Sweet dreams!

제 **꿈**은 한국에서 일하는 거예요. My dream is to work in Korea.

3 **다치다** *v.* **to get hurt, be injured**

어제 축구를 하다가 다리를 **다쳤어요**.
While playing soccer yesterday, I hurt my leg.

syn. 상처를 입다 **to get hurt**, 상처가 나다 **to get hurt** → 1-11

4 **도착(到着)** *n.* **arrival**
도착하다 [도차카다] *v.* **to arrive at**

도착 시간 arrival time

제가 지금 출발하면 1시까지 학교에 **도착할** 수 있어요.
If I leave now, I can arrive at school by 1:00.

비행기 **도착 시간**이 몇 시예요?
What is the arrival time of the flight?

ant. 출발 *n.* **departure**

5 **떠들다** *v.* **to chat, make a noise**

(ㄹ) 떠들어 – 떠듭니다 – 떠들 – 떠드는

수업 중에 **떠들지** 마세요. Don't chat during class.

아이들이 극장에서 시끄럽게 **떠듭니다**.
In the movie theatre, the kids are chatting loudly.

6 **마르다[2]** *v.* **to lose weight; to be thin, skinny, slim**

(르) 말라–마릅니다–마를–마르는

우리 집 강아지는 밥을 안 먹어서 너무 **말랐어요**.
Our dog does not eat food, so he is very skinny.

When 마르다 functions like an adjective to stand for being skinny, it should be used in the completed form. Thus, it should be 그 남자는 말랐어요 'That man is skinny.' or 마른 사람 'a skinny person'.

7 **물론(勿論)** *n./adv.* **(being) needless to say**

물론이에요./물론이지요. Of course.

가: 김 선생님 아세요? Do you know Mr. Kim?

나: **물론** 잘 알고 있습니다. Of course, I know him well.

8 **배우(俳優)** *n.* **actor, actress**

남자 배우 actor, 여배우 actress

저는 유명한 영화**배우**가 되고 싶어요.
I want to become a famous movie star.

9 **불편하다(不便–)** *adj.* **to be uncomfortable, inconvenient**

이 의자는 아주 **불편해요**. This chair is very uncomfortable.

이 도시는 교통이 **불편하네요**.
The transportation in this city is inconvenient.

ant. 편리하다 **to be convenient** →24-18,
편하다 **to be comfortable** →1-20

10 **사촌(四寸)** *n.* **cousin**

외사촌 *n.* cousin on the mother's side

현우는 제 **사촌** 동생이에요. Hyunwu is my (younger) cousin.

rel. 삼촌 *n.* **uncle**

11 **세계(世界)** *n.* **the world**

제2차 세계대전 World War II

세계적인 world famous

꼭 **세계** 여행을 해 보고 싶어요.
I really want to take a trip around the world.

싸이는 **세계적인** 가수가 됐어요. Psy became a world famous singer.

syn. 세계 *n.* **the world, society**

12 **시끄럽다** *adj.* **to be noisy**

(ㅂ) 시끄러워 – 시끄럽습니다 – 시끄러울 – 시끄러운

방이 길 옆에 있어서 너무 **시끄러워요.**
Because my room is next to the street, it is very noisy.

ant. 조용하다 *adj.* **to be quiet** → 24-16

13 **썰다** *v.* **to cut, slice, chop (usually with a knife)**

(ㄹ) 썰어 – 썹니다 – 썰 – 써는

양파를 **썰** 때 어떻게 하면 눈물이 안 나요?
When you cut an onion, what can I do so my eyes won't tear up?

rel. 자르다 *v.* **to cut, slice** → Appendix E

14 **어울리다** *v.* **to fit, go along well; to socialize**

저한테 제일 잘 **어울리는** 색깔이 뭐예요? What color suits me best?

요즘 누구하고 자주 **어울려요**?
Lately, who do you frequently hang out with?

어울리다 is used with many particles to make phrases such as (누구)한테 잘 어울리다 to fit on (someone), to suit or (무엇/누구)하고 어울리다 to match well with (something/someone), (누구)하고 자주 어울리다 to socialize, hang out with (someone).

15 **우체국(郵遞局)** *n.* **post office**

이번 토요일이 아빠 생신이라서 **우체국**에 가서 선물을 보냈다.
Because this Saturday is my dad's birthday, I sent him a birthday present at the post office.

rel. 우체통 *n.* **mailbox**, 우체부 *n.* **mailman**

16 입구(入口) [입꾸] *n.* **entrance**

가: 어디서 만날까? Where should we meet?

나: 지하철역 **입구**에서 만나자.
Let's meet at the entrance to the subway station.

ant. 출구 *n.* exit

17 정말 *adv.* **really;** *n.* **truth, reality**

엄마, 이 음식 **정말** 맛있어요. Mom, this food is really delicious.

이건 제가 만들었어요. **정말**이에요.
I made this. It is true./I am not lying.

syn. 참 *adv.* really, truly, 아주 *adv.* very → 6-14

18 직접(直接) [직쩝] *adv.* **directly, in person, personally**

집에서 학교까지 **직접** 가는 버스가 없어요.
There is no bus that goes directly from my house to school.

이 쿠키 맛있지 않아요? 제가 **직접** 만들었습니다.
Aren't these cookies delicious? I made them myself.

19 통화(通話) *n.* **phone call**
통화하다 *v.* **to talk over the phone**

통화 중이다 The line is busy; somebody is on the phone.

피터한테 계속 전화하는데 **통화**가 안 돼요.
I keep calling Peter but he doesn't answer the phone.

지금 나 너무 바빠. 미안한데 우리 다음에 **통화하자**.
I am busy now. I'm sorry but let's talk over the phone later.

20 휴일(休日) *n.* **holiday, day off**

미국에서는 9월 초에 **휴일**이 하루 있어서 좋아요.
In the United States, it is good that there is one day off in early September.

rel. 공휴일 *n.* legal holiday

CHECK UP

꿈, 물론, 배우, 사촌, 세계, 우체국, 입구, 정말, 직접, 휴일

1 actor, actress ______

2 cousin ______

3 directly, in person ______

4 dream ______

5 entrance ______

6 holiday, day off ______

7 needless to say ______

8 post office ______

9 really, real story ______

10 the world ______

CHECK UP

계획하다, 다치다, 도착하다, 떠들다, 마르다, 불편하다, 시끄럽다,
썰다, 어울리다, 통화하다

1 to arrive at ______________

2 to be noisy ______________

3 to be uncomfortable ______________

4 to chat, make a noise ______________

5 to cut, slice ______________

6 to fit, go along well ______________

7 to get hurt ______________

8 to lose weight, be skinny ______________

9 to plan ______________

10 to talk over the phone ______________

직업 Jobs 1

가수 singer

감독 director, 방송국 피디 director (*lit.* Broadcasting station producer), 프로듀서 producer

건축가 architect

경찰관 policeman

과학자 scientist

교사 teacher, 선생님 teacher

교수 professor

군인 soldier / military person

기자 reporter

미술가 artist

미용사 hairdresser, 이발사 barber

배우 actor

변호사 lawyer, 검사 prosecutor, 판사 judge

사업가 businessman, entrepreneur, 사장 company CEO, 회장 chairman

사진사, 사진작가 photographer

LESSON 22

1 고향(故鄕) *n.* hometown; home country; one's birth place

고향이 어디세요? What is your hometown?

한국은 나의 제2의 고향이야. Korea is my second home.

2 끝 *n.* end

차들이 너무 많아서 끝이 보이지 않네요.

There are too many cars, so we cannot see an end (of the traffic).

끝 is often used in the verbal form and there are two common forms: (~이/가) 끝나다 (event) to be over vs. (~을/를) 끝내다 (person) to finish. Note that the particle used in each phrase is different from each other.

한국어 수업이 몇 시에 **끝나요**? What time does the Korean class end?

저는 밤 11시에 숙제를 **끝냈어요**. I finished my homework at 11:00 pm.

ant. 시작 *n.* beginning ⋯24-11

3 닦다 *v.* to clean, wipe, wash, polish

구두를 닦다 to polish one's shoes

자기 전에 이를 꼭 닦으세요.

Make sure to brush your teeth before you go to bed.

rel. 씻다 *v.* to wash ⋯1-14

4 독서(讀書) [독써] *n.* reading books
독서하다 [독써하다] *v.* to read books

한국에서는 가을을 독서의 계절이라고 해요.

In Korea, people say autumn is the reading season.

저는 취미가 독서예요. My hobby is reading books.

syn. 책읽기 *n.* reading books

5 떨어지다 [떠러지다] *v.* to fall, drop

병이 테이블에서 떨어져서 깨졌어요.

The bottle fell from the table and broke.

오늘은 어제보다 기온이 많이 떨어졌어요.

The temperature dropped a lot today compared to yesterday.

For describing something or someone falling from a standing position, 넘어지다 'to fall, trip over' is used.

저는 달리기를 하다가 **넘어졌어요**. I fell down while running.

6 먼저 — *adv.* **in advance, first, earlier**

먼저 가세요. Please go first.

한국에서는 식사할 때 어른보다 **먼저** 먹으면 안돼요.

When you eat in Korea, you should not eat before your senior(s).

ant. 나중에 *adv.* later, 이따가 *adv.* (just a little) later

7 미래(未來) — *n.* **future**

한국어를 열심히 공부하면 **미래**가 밝을 거예요.

If you study Korean well, your future will be bright.

rel. 과거 *n.* past, 현재 *n.* present

8 배우다 — *v.* **to learn, take lessons**

이번 여름 방학에는 운전을 꼭 **배울** 거예요.

This summer vacation, I will learn how to drive.

ant. 가르치다 *v.* to teach → 4-1

9 붓다[1] [붇따] — *v.* **to swell, become swollen**

(ㅅ) 부어요 - 붓습니다 - 부을 - 붓는

축구를 하다가 다쳐서 발목이 **부었어요**.

I got injured while I was playing soccer, so my ankle is swollen.

너무 울어서 눈이 **부은** 것 같아요.

I cried so much that my eyes seems to be swollen.

10 산(山) — *n.* **mountain**

등산 mountain climbing

한국에서 제일 높은 **산**은 백두산이에요.

The tallest mountain in Korea is Mt. *Baekdu*.

rel. (산)정상, 산꼭대기 *n.* top of a mountain

11 **세수하다(洗手–)** 세수

v. **to wash one's face**
n. **washing one's face**

저는 아침에 일어나서 바로 이를 닦고 **세수해요**.
Right after I get up, I brush my teeth and wash my face.
날씨가 더워서 찬물로 **세수했어요**.
Because the weather is hot, I washed my face with cold water.

rel. 양치질하다 *v.* **to brush one's teeth** (=이를 닦다), 목욕하다 *v.* **to take a bath**

12 **시내(市内)**

n. **downtown, intra-city**

시내 버스 *n.* intra-city bus
버스나 지하철을 타면 서울 **시내**를 편하게 다닐 수 있다.
If you take the bus or the subway, you can get around easily in Seoul.

13 **쓰다**[1]

(으) 써–쓰니다–쓸–쓰는

v. **to write**

쓰기 *n.* writing
요즘은 편지를 **쓰지** 않아요. 전화를 하거나 문자를 보내죠.
These days, we don't write letters. We make calls or send texts.

14 **쓰레기**

n. **trash, waste**

쓰레기통 trash can
한국에서는 음식물 **쓰레기**는 따로 버려야 해요.
In Korea, food waste has to be disposed separately.

rel. 휴지 *n.* **trash paper; tissue, toilet paper** →24-19

15 **얼다**

(ㄹ) 얼어–업니다–얼–어는

v. **to freeze**

얼음 *n.* ice
지난 겨울에 너무 추워서 한강이 **얼었어요**.
It was so cold last winter that the Han River froze.
오늘 날씨가 더우니까 커피에 **얼음**을 넣어 주세요.
Because it is hot today, please put some ice in my coffee.

Note that 얼음 should not be misspelled as 어름.

16 운동(運動)
운동하다

n. **sports, exercise**
v. **to exercise**

운동복 sportswear, 운동 선수 athlete, 운동장 playground, 운동화 sneakers

저는 보통 일주일에 네 번씩 **운동**을 해요.
I usually exercise four times a week.

17 입원하다(入院－)

v. **to be hospitalized**

할머니께서 편찮으셔서 병원에 며칠 동안 **입원하셨어요**.
My grandmother was very sick, so she was hospitalized for a few days.

ant. 퇴원하다 *v.* **to be discharged from the hospital**

18 제일(第一)

n./adv. **the first, the most**

제가 **제일** 좋아하는 계절은 겨울이에요. (= 저는 겨울이 **제일** 좋아요.)
My favorite season is winter.

소현이는 저하고 **제일** 친한 친구예요. Sohyeon is my best friend.

더울 때는 아이스크림이 **제일**이에요.
When it is hot, icecream is the best.

Note that 제일 친구 is not a grammatical phrase.

syn. 가장 *adv.* **most, best**

19 질문(質問)
질문하다

n. **question**
v. **to ask a question**

수업 시간에 **질문**이 있으면 손을 드세요.
If you have any questions in class, raise your hand.

Note that 질문을 물어보다 is not a natural expression.

rel. 물어보다 *v.* **to ask**

20 특히(特－) [트키]

adv. **particularly, especially**

나는 한국 음식을 좋아해요. **특히** 갈비가 제일 좋아요.
I like Korean food. Particularly, *kalbi* is my favorite food.

syn. 특별히 *adv.* **particularly, especially**

CHECK UP

고향, 끝, 먼저, 미래, 산, 시내, 쓰레기, 운동, 제일, 특히

1 downtown, intra-city ______

2 end ______

3 future ______

4 hometown ______

5 in advance, first ______

6 mountain ______

7 particularly, especially ______

8 sports, exercise ______

9 the first, the most ______

10 trash, waste ______

CHECK UP

닦다, 독서하다, 떨어지다, 배우다, 붓다, 세수하다, 쓰다, 얼다, 입원하다, 질문하다

1 to ask a question ____________

2 to clean, wipe, wash, polish ____________

3 to fall, drop ____________

4 to freeze ____________

5 to be hospitalized ____________

6 to learn, take lessons ____________

7 to read books ____________

8 to swell, become swollen ____________

9 to wash one's face ____________

10 to write ____________

직업 Jobs 2

(운동)선수 sports player, athlete

소방관 firefighter

소설가 novelist

엔지니어 engineer

연예인 entertainer

요리사 cook / chef

우주비행사 astronaut

운전사/기사 driver

음악가 musician

연주자 instrument player: 바이올리니스트 violinist, 피아니스트 pianist

의사 doctor, 약사 pharmacist, 간호사 nurse, 수의사 veterinarian

작가 writer

정치인/정치가 politician, 대통령 president,
국회의원 member of the National Assembly, congressman

주부 homemaker

컴퓨터 프로그래머 computer programmer

화가 artist

회계사 accountant

회사원 company employee

LESSON 23

1 **공원(公園)** *n.* **park**

국립 공원 national park

저는 매일 아침 집 근처 **공원**에서 산책해요.
Every morning, I take a walk at the park near my house.

2 **나가다** *v.* **to go out**

저희 오빠는 친구를 만나러 **나갔어요**.
My older brother went out to see his friend.

rel. 나오다 *v.* **to come out**

저는 오늘 아침 집에서 8시에 나왔어요.
I came out of my house at 8:00 in the morning.

3 **닫다** *v.* **to close, shut**

닫히다 to be closed (passive form of 닫다)

창문 좀 **닫아** 주세요.
Please close the window.

바람에 문이 **닫혔어요**.
The door was closed by the wind.

Note that 닫다 is a regular verb and does not conjugate like other ㄷ–ending words like 듣다–들어요–들을 'to listen to' or 걷다–걸어요–걸을 'to walk'.

ant. 열다 *v.* **to open** → 6-15

4 **돈** *n.* **money**

돈을 내다 to pay money, 돈을 벌다 to make or earn money, 돈을 찾다 to withdraw money (from the bank), 돈을 쓰다 to spend money, 돈을 빌리다 to borrow money, 거스름돈 change (money)

죄송하지만 **돈** 좀 빌려 주세요.
I am sorry, but please lend me some money.

저는 **돈을 찾으러** 은행에 가요.
I am going to the bank to withdraw money.

Note that 돈을 만들다 is not a common expression for 'to earn/make money' because it may stand for 'to make coins or bills'.

5 **등산(登山)**
등산하다

n. **hiking, mountain climbing**
v. **to hike, climb mountain**

등산객 mountain climber

우리 아버지는 매주 일요일에 **등산**을 가세요.
My father goes hiking every Sunday.

6 **똑바로 [똑빠로]**

adv. **straight, upright, correctly, right**

똑바로 앉으세요. Please sit up.

가: 실례지만 지하철역이 어디에 있어요?
Excuse me, but where is the subway station?

나: 이 길로 **똑바로** 가세요.
Go straight ahead this way.

rel. 쭉 *adv.* **straight; all the time** ···24-17

7 **멀다**

adj. **to be far**

(ㄹ) 멀어 –
멉니다 – 멀 – 먼

우리 집이 학교에서 너무 **먼** 것 같아요.
It seems that my home is too far from the school.

가: 한국어를 잘 하시네요!
You speak Korean well!

나: 아니에요. 아직 **멀었어요**. No. I am not that good yet. (*lit.* It is still far from reaching that level.)

ant. 가깝다 *adj.* **to be close** ···2-1

8 **미리**

adv. **in advance, ahead of time**

한국 여행을 하려면 **미리** 계획을 해야 해요.
If you want to travel to Korea, you must plan in advance.

늦으면 **미리** 연락해 주세요.
If you are delayed, please contact me ahead of time.

9 **백화점(百貨店)**
[배콰점]

n. **department store**

저는 내일 오후에 **백화점**에 쇼핑하러 가요.
Tomorrow afternoon, I will go to the department store to shop.

백화점 is different from 쇼핑몰 'shopping mall'.

10 버리다 | *v.* to throw away

쓰레기를 버리지 마세요.
No littering.
한국에서는 음식물 쓰레기는 따로 버려야 해요.
In Korea, food waste should be disposed separately.

When 버리다 is used after other verb in the structure of '~어/아 버리다', its function is to indicate that the action ended up in an irrevocable situation.

우리 개가 제 숙제를 다 먹어 **버렸어요**. Our dog ate up my homework.
약속을 잊어 **버렸어요**. I (completely) forgot the appointment.

11 붓다[2] [붇따] | *v.* to pour, put (liquid)

(ㅅ) 부어 – 붓습니다 – 부을 – 붓는

주스를 잔에 부어 주세요.
Please, pour the juice in the glass.

12 세우다 | *v.* to stop; to park (a vehicle); to make someone/something stop

기사 아저씨, 여기서 좀 세워 주세요.
Mr. Driver, please stop the car here.
집 앞에 차를 세워도 돼요?
Can I park my car in front of your house?

rel. 서다 *v.* to stand → 9-11

13 시원하다 | *adj.* to be cool; to be refreshing

여름에도 아침에는 좀 시원해요.
Even in summer, it's quite cool in the morning.

ant. 따뜻하다 *adj.* to be warm, *rel.* 덥다 *adj.* to be hot

14 여권(旅券) [여꿘] | *n.* passport

외국에 가려면 여권이 있어야 한다.
In order to go abroad, you must have a passport.

rel. 비자 *n.* visa

15 **운전하다(運轉–)** *v.* **to drive**
운전 *n.* **driving**

운전 기사 driver, 운전 면허 driver's license

저는 기숙사에 살아서 **운전하지** 않아도 돼요.
Because I live in a dormitory, I don't have to drive.

집에서 학교까지 **운전해서** 20분쯤 걸려요.
From my house to school, it takes about 20 minutes when I drive.

16 **입학(入學) [이팍]** *n.* **admission to a school; entrance into a school**
입학하다 [이파카다] *v.* **to be admitted to a school**

초등학교에 **입학한** 지 벌써 10년도 넘었어요.
It has already been more than 10 years since I entered elementary school.

ant. 졸업 *n.* **graduation**

17 **조금** *adv.* **little,** *n.* **a little amount**

오늘은 집에 일찍 가야겠어요. 머리가 **조금** 아파요.
I have to go home early today. I have a mild headache. (*lit.* My head is in a bit of pain.)

In colloquial speech, it is often pronounced with tense sounds as [쪼끔].

syn. 좀 *adv.* **a little; please**

18 **짧다 [짤따]** *adj.* **to be short**

작년에 산 바지가 올해는 좀 **짧아졌어요**.
The pants that I bought last year are shorter this year.

Note that 짧다 should not be used for describing a person's height. For that meaning, you should say 키가 작다.

ant. 길다 *adj.* **to be long** → 18-2

19 **팔다** *v.* **to sell**

(ㄹ) 팔아 – 팝니다 – 팔 – 파는

신발을 사러 왔는데 여기 양말도 **팔아요**?
I came here to buy shoes. Do you sell socks, too?
동대문 시장에서는 옷을 싸게 **팝니다**.
At *Dongdaemun* market, they sell clothes for cheap.

ant. 사다 *v.* **to buy** →12-10

20 **흐리다** *adj.* **to be cloudy, muddy** →3-3

흐려지다 to become cloudy
오늘은 좀 **흐리고** 바람이 불겠습니다.
It's going to be cloudy and windy today.
하늘이 **흐려지고** 비가 내리기 시작했습니다.
The sky became cloudy and started to rain.

syn. 구름이 끼다 *v.* **to be couldy**, *ant.* 맑다 *adj.* **to be clear**, *rel.* 구름 *n.* **cloud**, 햇빛 *n.* **sunlight**

CHECK UP

공원, 돈, 등산, 똑바로, 미리, 백화점, 여권, 운전, 입학, 조금

1 admission to a school; entrance into a school ....

2 department store ....

3 driving ....

4 hiking, mountain climbing ....

5 in advance ....

6 little ....

7 money ....

8 park ....

9 passport ....

10 straight, upright ....

CHECK UP

나가다, 닫다, 멀다, 버리다, 붓다, 세우다, 시원하다, 짧다, 팔다, 흐리다

1 to be cloudy ____________

2 to be cool, refreshing ____________

3 to be far ____________

4 to be short ____________

5 to close, shut ____________

6 to go out ____________

7 to pour, put ____________

8 to sell ____________

9 to stop, to park (a vehicle) ____________

10 to throw away ____________

LESSON 24

1 공항(空港) *n.* airport

국제 공항 international airport, 공항 버스 airport limousine bus
죄송하지만 **공항**까지 좀 태워 주실 수 있어요?
I am sorry, but can you give me a ride to the airport?

rel. 국제선 *n.* international lines, 국내선 *n.* domestic lines, 항공 *n.* flight, aviation

2 나라 *n.* country, nation

우리 나라 my country
어느 **나라** 사람이세요? What country are you from?

syn. 국가 *n.* country, nation

3 달다 *adj.* to taste sweet

(ㄹ) 달아 – 답니다 – 달 – 단

이 케이크는 너무 **달아요**. This cake is too sweet.
단 음식을 너무 많이 먹으면 살이 쪄요.
If you eat too many sweet foods, you will gain weight.

rel. 짜다 *adj.* to be salty, 맵다 *adj.* to be spicy → 20-6, 시다 *adj.* to be sour, 쓰다 *adj.* to be bitter

4 돌 *n.* one's first birthday

돌잔치 the birthday party for one's one-year-old baby
조카의 **돌** 선물로 금반지를 샀어요.
For my nephew's first birthday, I bought him a gold ring.

5 뛰다 *v.* to run, dash; to jump

저는 오늘 늦게 일어나서 수업에 **뛰어** 왔어요.
I woke up late today, so I ran to class.
얘들아, 침대 위에서 **뛰면** 안 돼. Kids, you should not jump on the bed.

Both 달리다 'to run' and 뛰다 can be used to describe the movement of people, animals or cars, while 뛰다 can only be used for people or animals. → 1-4

6 **멋있다**
[머싣따/머딛따]

adj. **to be stylish, cool, fashionable**

우리 선생님이 너무 **멋있으시지요**?
Our teacher is really cool, right?
너 오늘 옷이 너무 **멋있어**.
Your clothes look great today.

7 **미용실(美容室)**

n. **beauty shop, hairdresser's**

저는 내일 머리하러 **미용실**에 갈 거예요.
I am going to the beauty shop tomorrow to get my hair done.

syn. 미장원 *n.* **beauty shop**, *rel.* 이발소 *n.* **barber shop**

8 **붙다 [붇따]**

v. **to stick to, adhere to; to pass (an exam)**

신발에 껌이 **붙었어요**. I've got gum stuck to my shoe.
저는 어제 운전 면허 시험에 **붙었습니다**.
I passed my driver's license test yesterday.

rel. 붙이다 *v.* **to stick, attach** →25-9

9 **살다**

(ㄹ) 살아-
삽니다-살-사는

v. **to live**

저는 학교 근처에 **살아요**. I live near school.
노아는 졸업하고 한국에서 **산대요**.
Noah said he is going to live in Korea after he graduates.

ant. 죽다 *v.* **to die** →10-18

10 **세탁 (洗濯)**
세탁하다 [세타카다]

n. **washing clothes**
v. **to wash clothes**

세탁기 washing machine, 세탁소 dry cleaner's
다음 주에 인터뷰가 있어요. 정장을 **세탁해야** 돼요.
I have an interview next week. I have to wash my suits.

While 세탁하다 is used in more professional context, 빨래하다 is generally used in every day conversations.

rel. 빨래 *n.* **laundry** →7-10

11 시작
시작하다 [시자카다]

n. **beginning, start**
v. **to begin, start**

한국어 수업은 몇 시에 **시작해요**?
What time does the Korean class begin?

ant. 끝 *n.* **end**, 끝나다 *v.* **to be over** →22-2

12 쓰다[2]

v. **to use**

요즘 많은 사람들은 집전화를 안 **쓰고** 스마트폰만 **써요**.
Lately, many people are using smartphones and not a home phone.
수업 시간에 영어를 **쓰지** 마세요.
Do not use English in class.

syn. 사용하다 →16-10, 이용하다 *v.* **to use**

13 여행(旅行)
여행하다

n. **travel, trip**
v. **to travel**

여행(을) 가다 to take a trip, 여행사 travel agency
Please compare the following sentences:
이번 여름 방학에는 한국에서 **여행**을 할 거예요.
During this summer vacation, I will travel around Korea.
이번 여름 방학에는 한국에 **여행 갈** 거예요.
This summer vacation, I will travel to Korea.

14 울다

v. **cry**

(ㄹ) 울어-웁니다-울-우는

울음 crying
울리다 to make somebody cry
사람들이 **우는** 아이를 도와줍니다.
People help kids that are crying.
현우는 어렸을 때 동생을 자주 **울렸어요**.
When he was younger, Hyeonwu often made his younger brother cry.

ant. 웃다 *v.* **to smile, laugh** →25-15

15 있다 — *v.* **to be, exist; to have, possess**

우리 집 앞에 작은 약국이 **있어요**.
There is a small pharmacy in front of my house.

집에 **있는** 제 강아지가 보고 싶어요.
I want to see my puppy at home.

Two equivalent Korean structures of English 'to be, exist' and 'to have' are identical. Note that in Korean 있다, even when it stands for 'to have', always requires a noun that is associated with a subject marker '–이/가' instead of an object marker '–을/를' as in English.

rel. 계시다 *v.* to be, exist (honorific) ···19-1

16 조용하다 — *adj.* **to be quiet, silent**

이 건물 안이 너무 **조용해요**. 좀 무서워요.
It is too quiet in this building. I'm a little scared.

ant. 시끄럽다 *adj.* to be noisy ···21-12

17 쭉 — *adv.* **straight; all the time**

도서관이요? 이 길로 **쭉** 가시면 왼쪽에 있어요.
The library? If you go straight on this street, you can find it your left.

저는 오늘 집에 **쭉** 있었어요. I stayed home all day today.

syn. 똑바로 *adv.* straight, correctly ···23-6

18 편리하다(便利–) [펼리하다] — *adj.* **to be convenient**

우리 집 옆에 지하철역이 있어서 아주 **편리해요**.
There is a subway station near my house, which is very convenient.

rel. 편하다 *adj.* to be comfortable ···1-20, *ant.* 불편하다 *v.* to be inconvenient; to be uncomfortable ···21-9

19 휴지(休紙) *n.* **wastepaper, garbage (paper); tissue, toilet paper**

휴지통 trash can

휴지는 꼭 가까운 휴지통에 넣어 주세요.
Please be sure to put your trash in a trash can near you.

화장실 **휴지**를 다 썼어요. The bathroom is out of toilet paper.

rel. 쓰레기 *n.* **trash, garbage** 22-14

20 힘 *n.* **strength, energy, force**

힘이 세다 to be strong

제 남동생은 몸은 작은데 **힘이 세요**.
My brother is small, but he is strong.

감기에 걸려서 온 몸에 **힘**이 하나도 없어요.
I caught a cold so I don't have any strength.

rel. 힘들다 *adj.* **to be hard, tough; to be difficult** 25-20

CHECK UP

공항, 나라, 돌, 미용실, 세탁, 시작, 여행, 쭉, 휴지, 힘

1 airport ....

2 beauty shop ....

3 beginning ....

4 country, nation ....

5 one's first birthday ....

6 straight, all the time ....

7 strength ....

8 travel ....

9 washing clothes, laundry ....

10 wastepaper; tissue ....

CHECK UP

달다, 뛰다, 멋있다, 붙다, 살다, 쓰다, 울다, 있다, 조용하다, 편리하다

1 to be convenient ______________________

2 to be quiet ______________________

3 to be stylish ______________________

4 to cry ______________________

5 to exist; to have ______________________

6 to live ______________________

7 to run, jump ______________________

8 to stick to, to pass an exam ______________________

9 to taste sweet ______________________

10 to use ______________________

LESSON 25

1 **과일** *n.* **fruit** ⋯ Appendix G

과일 가게 fruit store

건강을 위해서 매일 **과일**을 먹어야 돼요.

For the sake of your health, you need to eat fruits every day.

rel. 야채, 채소 *n.* **vegetable**

2 **나무** *n.* **tree; wood**

나무를 심다 to plant trees

이 공원에는 큰 **나무**들이 많이 있어요.

There are many big trees in this park.

이 가구는 **나무**로 만들었어요. This furniture is made of wood.

3 **달력 (-曆)** *n.* **calendar**

중요한 날은 모두 **달력**에 적어 놓으세요.

Write down all important days on the calendar.

요즘은 인터넷에 있는 **달력**이 참 편리해요.

These days the internet's calendar is really convenient to use.

4 **돌다** *v.* **to turn**

(ㄹ) 돌아 – 돕니다 – 돌 – 도는

돌아가다 to turn back, go back, 돌아오다 to return, come back, 돌아가시다 to die, pass away (honorific form of 죽다)

저 사거리에서 왼쪽으로 **도세요**. Turn left at that intersection.

제 친구는 고향으로 **돌아갔어요**.

My friend went back to his hometown.

룸메이트가 여행을 갔다가 내일 **돌아올** 거예요.

My roommate went on a trip, and will be back tomorrow.

저희 할아버지께서는 작년에 **돌아가셨어요**.

My grandfather passed away last year.

5 **뜨겁다** *adj.* **to be hot, burning**

(ㅂ) 뜨거워 – 뜨겁습니다 – 뜨거울 – 뜨거운

뜨거운 커피를 마시면서 운전하면 위험해요.

It is dangerous to drive while drinking hot coffee.

커피가 아주 **뜨거워요**. 조심하세요.

The coffee is really hot. Be careful.

The hotness of objects should be described with 뜨겁다 while 덥다 'to be hot' is generally used for describing air temperature. ···› 16-4

ant. 차갑다 *adj.* to be cold

6 메다

v. to carry something on one's shoulder

가방을 메다 to carry a bag

제 친구는 배낭을 **메고** 학교에 갔어요.
My friend shouldered her backpack and went to school.

7 밀리다

v. to be left undone

숙제가 **밀려서** 주말에는 도서관에 가야겠어요. I am behind in my homework, so I should go to the library this weekend.

주말에는 보통 **밀린** 빨래를 해요.
I do my piled-up laundry on weekends.

rel. 밀다 *v.* to push

8 벌써

adj. already

버스가 **벌써** 떠났어요? 학교에 늦겠어요.
Did the bus leave already? I guess I will be late for school.

ant. 아직 *adv.* (not) ... yet ···› 7-14

9 붙이다 [부치다]

v. to stick, attach, glue

벽에 포스터를 **붙이지** 마세요. Please don't attach posters on the wall.

봉투에 실수로 우표를 안 **붙였어요**.
By mistake, I didn't put a stamp on the envelope.

Compare with 부치다 'to send (a letter/money).' ···› 17-9

rel. 붙다 *v.* to stick ···› 24-8

10 상자(箱子)

n. box

이 사과는 한 **상자**에 이만 원이에요.
These apples are 20 thousand won a box.

이 나무 **상자** 안에 뭐가 들어 있어요? What is inside the wooden box?

syn. 박스 *n.* box

11 소개(紹介)
소개하다

n. **introduction**
v. **to introduce**

자기소개 *n.* self-introduction

제 **소개**를 해 드리겠습니다. Let me introduce myself.

안녕하십니까? 김 선생님 **소개**로 왔습니다.
Hello. I'm here at the recommendation of Prof. Kim.

옆에 계신 분 누구세요? 좀 **소개해** 주세요.
Who's the person next to you? Can you introduce him to us?

12 시장(市場)

n. **market, marketplace**

어머니는 **시장**에서 장을 봤어요.
My mother went grocery shopping at the marketplace.

시장 generally refers to traditional market. For modern style supermarkets, 슈퍼마켓, 슈퍼, 마켓, or 마트 are used.

13 씹다

v. **to chew**

꼭꼭 씹다 to chew thoroughly

꼭꼭 씹어 먹는 것이 건강에 좋아요.
It is good for your health to chew thoroughly.

수업 시간에는 껌을 **씹지** 마세요. Don't chew gum during class.

14 역(驛)

n. **(train or subway) station**

기차역 train station, 지하철역 subway station, 서울역 Seoul Station

시청에 가려면 다음 **역**에서 내리세요.
If you want to go to the City Hall, get off at the next station.

rel. 버스 정류장 *n.* **bus stop**

15 웃다

v. **to laugh, smile**

웃음 laughter

웃으면 복이 와요. **웃는** 게 좋아요.
If you laugh, luck will come your way. It is good to laugh.

자 사진 찍겠습니다. 모두 **웃으세요**!
I will take a picture now. Everyone, smile!

ant. 울다 *v.* **to cry** →24-14
rel. 웃기다 *v.* **to make someone laugh or smile**

16 잊다

v. **to forget**

가: 오늘 어디에서 만날까요? Where should we meet today?

나: 미안해요. 약속을 **잊어버렸어요**. 내일 만나도 돼요?
I'm sorry. I forgot about the appointment. Can we meet tomorrow?

The verb 잊다 is usually used as 잊어버리다, which indicates that something completely left your mind.

17 좁다

adj. **to be narrow**

나는 저녁마다 강아지하고 집 근처 **좁은** 길에서 산책해요.
I take a walk with my puppy through a narrow road near my house every evening.

ant. 넓다 *adj.* **to be wide; to be spacious** → 8-3

18 쯤

suf. **about, around**

우리 선생님은 나이가 서른 살**쯤** 되신 것 같아요.
Our teacher seems to be about 30 years old.

시카고에서 서울까지 비행기로 14시간**쯤** 걸려요.
From Chicago to Seoul, it takes about 14 hours by airplane.

rel. 정도 *n.* **about, around**

19 편지 (便紙)

n. **letter**

요즘은 사람들이 **편지**를 안 써요. 그냥 이메일이나 문자를 보내죠.
Nowadays people do not write letters. They just send emails or texts.

20 힘들다

(ㄹ) 힘들어 – 힘듭니다 – 힘들 – 힘든

adj. **to be hard, tough, laborious; to be difficult**

오늘은 아프니까 너무 **힘든** 일은 하지 마세요.
Since you don't feel good today, you should not work too hard.

가: 이번 학기 학교 생활 어때요? How's life going this semester?

나: 어려운 과목이 많아서 좀 **힘들어요**. Since there are many difficult courses, it's a little hard.

syn. 어렵다 *adj.* **to be difficult** → 18-14
rel. 힘 *n.* **strength** → 24-20

CHECK UP

과일, 나무, 달력, 벌써, 상자, 소개, 시장, 역, 쯤, 편지

1 about, around ____________

2 already ____________

3 box ____________

4 calendar ____________

5 fruit ____________

6 introduction ____________

7 letter ____________

8 market ____________

9 station ____________

10 tree, wood ____________

CHECK UP

돌다, 뜨겁다, 메다, 밀리다, 붙이다, 씹다, 웃다, 잊다, 좁다, 힘들다

1 to be hard, tough ____________________

2 to be hot, burning ____________________

3 to be left undone ____________________

4 to be narrow ____________________

5 to carry something on the shoulder ____________________

6 to chew ____________________

7 to forget ____________________

8 to laugh, smile ____________________

9 to stick, attach ____________________

10 to turn ____________________

REVIEW Exercises

Choose the one which is most appropriate in the blank.

1 사람들은 보통 새해에 새해 계획을 __________.

① 세워요 ② 돼요 ③ 해요 ④ 서요

2 안녕히 주무세요. 좋은 꿈 __________.

① 꾸세요 ② 하세요 ③ 보세요 ④ 받으세요

3 저는 어제 달리기를 하다가 __________.

① 떨어졌어요 ② 넘어졌어요 ③ 빠졌어요 ④ 내렸어요

4 지금 돈이 없어요. 그래서 은행에 돈을 __________ 가요.

① 만들러 ② 받으러 ③ 내러 ④ 찾으러

5 저는 열심히 일해서 돈을 많이 __________ 싶어요.

① 만들고 ② 벌고 ③ 빌리고 ④ 찾고

6 한국어 수업은 1시에 시작해서 1시 50분에 __________.

① 나와요 ② 다 해요 ③ 끝내요 ④ 끝나요

7 질문 있는 사람들은 선생님께 질문 __________.

① 하세요 ② 물으세요 ③ 물어 보세요 ④ 대답하세요

8 방이 좀 춥네요. 창문을 좀 __________.

① 도와 주세요 ② 열어 주세요 ③ 올려 주세요 ④ 닫아 주세요

9 우리 집 근처에 지하철 역이 있어서 아주 __________. 학교에 빨리 갈 수 있어요.

① 편리해요 ② 편안해요 ③ 불편해요 ④ 복잡해요

10 아이들이 침대 위에서 ________ 있어요.

① 뛰고 ② 달리고 ③ 앉고 ④ 눕고

11 제 친구는 배낭을 ________ 학교에 갔어요.

① 데리고 ② 쓰고 ③ 입고 ④ 메고

12 실수로 봉투에 우표를 안 ________.

① 부쳤어요 ② 붙었어요 ③ 붙였어요 ④ 붙어 있어요

13 할머니가 편찮으셔서 병원에 ________ 하셨어요.

① 진찰 ② 입원 ③ 퇴원 ④ 의사

14 동대문 시장에서는 옷을 싸게 ________

① 사요 ② 싸요 ③ 팔아요 ④ 비싸요

15 정원에 나무가 없어서 저는 봄에 나무를 ________.

① 만들 거예요 ② 심을 거예요 ③ 자를 거예요 ④ 자랄 거예요

Choose the one that can replace the underlined part.

16 제 취미는 책 읽는 것이에요. 주로 소설 책을 읽어요.

① 독서 ② 쓰기 ③ 책방에 가기 ④ 공부하기

17 민수는 잠 자기 전에 꼭 이를 닦아요.

① 세수를 해요 ② 양치질을 해요 ③ 얼굴을 씻어요 ④ 머리를 감아요

18 우리 엄마 요리는 정말 맛있어요.

① 벌써 ② 별로 ③ 이미 ④ 참

REVIEW Exercises

19 휴지는 꼭 여기에 버리세요.

① 나머지 ② 종이 ③ 쓰레기 ④ 화장품

20 제가 제일 좋아하는 사람은 우리 엄마예요.

① 아주 ② 처음 ③ 굉장히 ④ 가장

Choose the one that has the opposite meaning to the underlined part.

21 먼저 가세요. 저는 조금 이따가 갈게요.

① 나중에 ② 조금 ③ 전에 ④ 일찍

22 한국어를 열심히 공부하면 미래가 밝을 거예요.

① 해 ② 작년 ③ 지난 ④ 과거

23 비행기 도착 시간이 몇 시예요?

① 출근 ② 출발 ③ 퇴근 ④ 휴가

24 이 도시는 교통이 아주 불편해요.

① 편리해요 ② 편안해요 ③ 복잡해요 ④ 불안해요

25 저는 2년 후에 졸업할 거예요.

① 학업 ② 수업 ③ 입학 ④ 출근

Answer

1 ① 2 ① 3 ② 4 ④ 5 ② 6 ④ 7 ① 8 ④ 9 ① 10 ① 11 ④ 12 ③ 13 ② 14 ③
15 ② 16 ① 17 ② 18 ④ 19 ③ 20 ④ 21 ① 22 ④ 23 ② 24 ① 25 ③

APPENDIX

A 여행 필수품 : Travel Necessities

① **여행 가방** suitcase	② **모자** cap	③ **셔츠** shirt
④ **선글라스** sun glasses	⑤ **충전기** charger	⑥ **면도기** shaver
⑦ **양말** socks	⑧ **수건** towel	⑨ **전화기** cell phone
⑩ **속옷** underwear	⑪ **사진기** camera	⑫ **책** book
⑬ **여권** passport	⑭ **지도** map	⑮ **치약** toothpaste
⑯ **비누** soap	⑰ **휴지** tissue	

B 동물 1 : Animals 1

① 소 cow　　② 닭 chicken　　③ 돼지 pig

④ 개 dog　　⑤ 고양이 cat　　⑥ 토끼 rabbit

⑦ 여우 fox　　⑧ 다람쥐 chipmunk, squirrel　　⑨ 쥐 rat

⑩ 새 bird　　⑪ 양 lamb, sheep

C 동물 2 : Animals 2

① **동물원** zoo
② **사자** lion
③ **호랑이** tiger
④ **뱀** snake
⑤ **기린** giraffe
⑥ **코끼리** elephant
⑦ **얼룩말** zebra
⑧ **곰** bear
⑨ **하마** hippopotamus
⑩ **원숭이** monkey
⑪ **너구리** raccoon

D 밥상 : Korean Style Dining Table

① **상, 밥상** dining table ② **밥** (steamed) rice ③ **국** soup

④ **반찬** side dishes ⑤ **숟가락** spoon ⑥ **젓가락** chopsticks

⑦ **수저** silverware (spoon and chopsticks) ⑧ **찌개** stew

E 요리 : Cooking

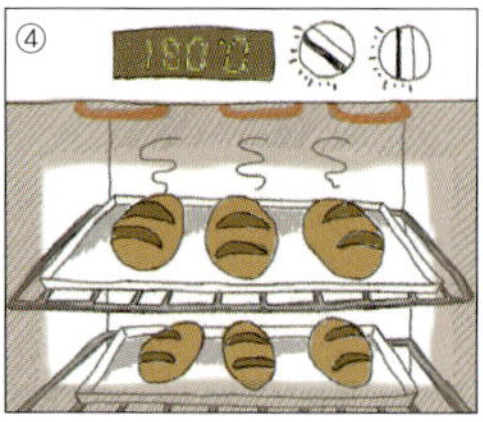

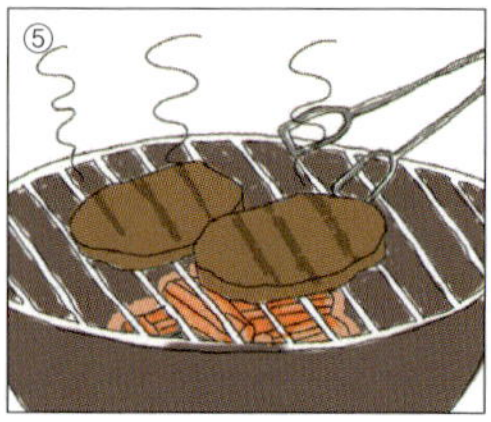

① **끓이다** to boil ② **볶다** to stir ③ **튀기다** to fry

④ **굽다** to bake ⑤ **굽다** to grill ⑥ **삶다** to boil

⑦ **찌다** to steam ⑧ **썰다** to slice, chop ⑨ **다지다** to mince

⑩ **자르다** to cut ⑪ **뿌리다** to sprinkle ⑫ **섞다** to stir, mix

⑬ **깎다** to peel

F 거리 : Street

① **사거리** intersection	② **인도, 보도** sidewalk	③ **버스정류장** bus stop
④ **버스** bus	⑤ **횡단보도** crosswalk	⑥ **차선** lane
⑦ **가로수** (roadside) tree	⑧ **중앙선** centerline	⑨ **가로등** streetlight
⑩ **신호등** traffic light	⑪ **지하철역** subway station	⑫ **육교** (pedestrian) overpass
⑬ **자동차** car	⑭ **도로** road	

G 채소, 과일 : Vegetables, Fruits

① **호박** zucchini, pumpkin
② **시금치** spinach
③ **상추** lettuce
④ **오이** cucumber
⑤ **마늘** garlic
⑥ **무** radish
⑦ **배추** napa cabbage
⑧ **양배추** cabbage
⑨ **파** scallion, green onion
⑩ **양파** onion
⑪ **당근** carrot
⑫ **배** pear
⑬ **감** persimmon
⑭ **복숭아** peach
⑮ **사과** apple
⑯ **딸기** strawberry
⑰ **포도** grape
⑱ **수박** watermelon

H 옷장 : Closet

① **치마** skirt ② **원피스** dress ③ **코트** coat

④ **점퍼** jacket ⑤ **티셔츠** t-shirt ⑥ **청바지** jeans

⑦ **와이셔츠** dress shirts ⑧ **스웨터** sweater ⑨ **장갑** gloves

⑩ **벨트** belt ⑪ **양말** socks ⑫ **스타킹** stockings

⑬ **옷걸이** (clothes) hanger

교통 수단 : Transportations

① **버스** bus
② **택시** taxi
③ **지하철** subway
④ **자전거** bicycle
⑤ **자동차** car
⑥ **오토바이** motorcycle
⑦ **스쿠터** scooter
⑧ **기차** train
⑨ **배** ship
⑩ **비행기** airplane

J 스포츠 : Sports

① 축구 soccer
② 농구 basketball
③ 야구 baseball
④ 배구 volleyball
⑤ 수영 swimming
⑥ 권투 boxing
⑦ 골프 golf
⑧ 미식축구 American football
⑨ 달리기 running
⑩ 탁구 ping pong

K 방 : Room

① 방 room	② 책상 desk	③ 의자 chair
④ 컴퓨터 computer	⑤ 침대 bed	⑥ 베개 pillow
⑦ 옷장 closet	⑧ 책꽂이 bookshelf	⑨ 창문 window
⑩ 거울 mirror	⑪ 벽시계 clock	⑫ 벽 wall
⑬ 바닥 floor		

L 가족 : Family

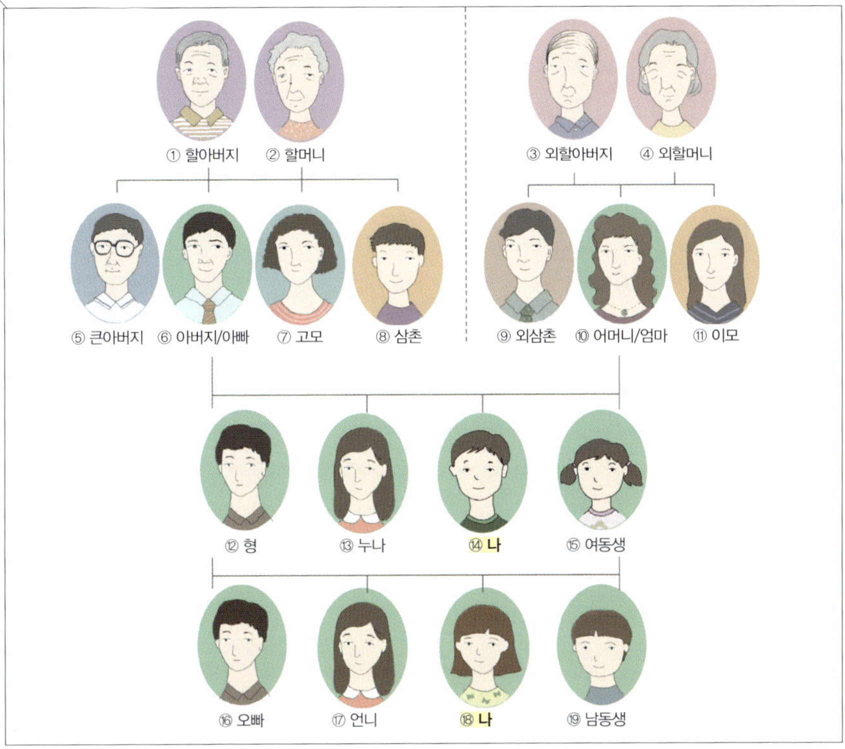

① **할아버지** grandfather
② **할머니** grandmother
③ **외할아버지** (mother's side) grandfather
④ **외할머니** (mother's side) grandmother
⑤ **큰아버지** uncle (father's older brother)
⑥ **아버지/아빠** father/dad
⑦ **고모** aunt (father's sister)
⑧ **삼촌** uncle (father's younger brother)
⑨ **외삼촌** uncle (mother's brother)
⑩ **어머니/엄마** mother/mom
⑪ **이모** aunt (mother's sister)
⑫ **형** older brother for a male
⑬ **누나** older sister for a male
⑭ **나** I (male)
⑮ **여동생** younger sister
⑯ **오빠** older brother for a female
⑰ **언니** older sister for a female
⑱ **나** I (female)
⑲ **남동생** younger brother

M 색깔 : Colors

① **빨간색/빨강** red
② **파란색/파랑** blue
③ **노란색/노랑** yellow
④ **흰색/하얀색** white
⑤ **검은색/검정색** black
⑥ **회색** gray
⑦ **주황색** orange
⑧ **초록색** green
⑨ **남색** indigo
⑩ **보라색** purple
⑪ **갈색** brown
⑫ **분홍색** pink

N 남자 옷, 신발, 액세서리 : Clothes, Shoes, Accessories for Men

① 안경 glasses ② 넥타이 necktie ③ 시계 watch, clock

④ 양말 socks ⑤ 반팔 셔츠 short sleeves shirt

⑥ 반바지 shorts ⑦ 모자 cap, hat ⑧ 목도리 scarf

⑨ 허리띠, 벨트 belt ⑩ 장화 rain boots ⑪ 와이셔츠 dress shirts

⑫ 자켓 jacket ⑬ 구두 dress shoes ⑭ 바지 pants

⑮ 우산 umbrella

여자 옷, 신발, 액세서리 : Clothes, Shoes, Accessories for Women

① **선글라스** sunglasses	② **스카프** scarf	③ **장갑** gloves
④ **반지** ring	⑤ **벨트** belt	⑥ **양말** socks
⑦ **가방** bag	⑧ **모자** hat, cap	⑨ **목걸이** necklace
⑩ **귀걸이** earring	⑪ **원피스** dress	⑫ **구두** dress shoes
⑬ **양산** parasol	⑭ **자켓** jacket	⑮ **부츠** boots

P 몸 1 : Body Parts 1

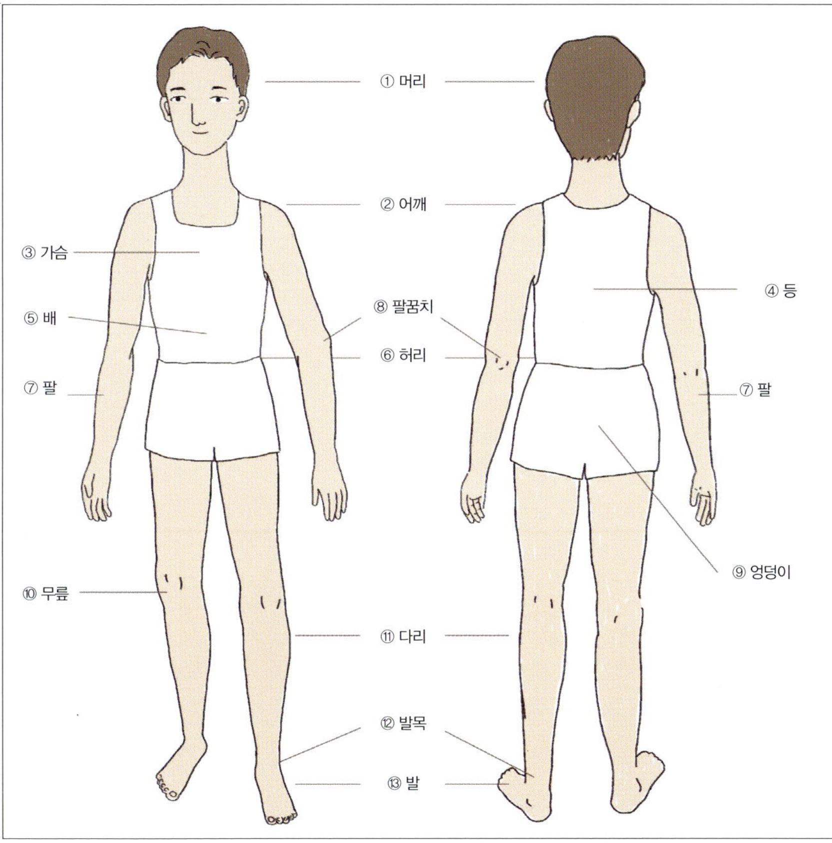

① **머리** head	② **어깨** shoulder	③ **가슴** chest
④ **등** back	⑤ **배** stomach	⑥ **허리** waist
⑦ **팔** arm	⑧ **팔꿈치** elbow	⑨ **엉덩이** buttocks
⑩ **무릎** knee	⑪ **다리** leg	⑫ **발목** ankle
⑬ **발** foot		

Q 몸 2 : Body Parts 2

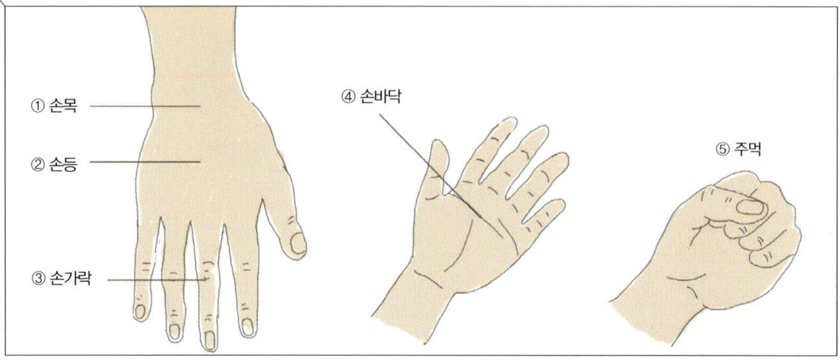

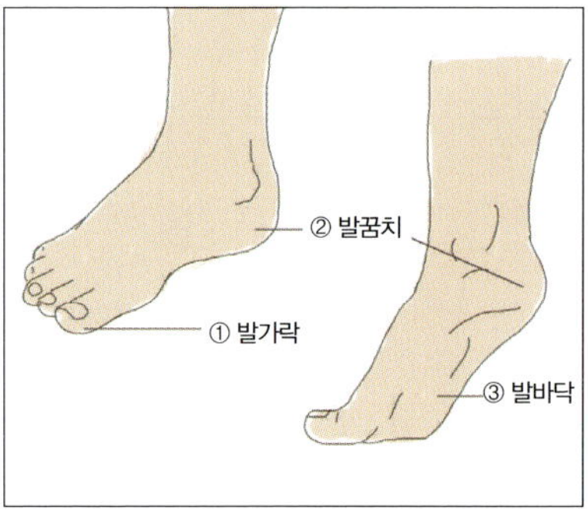

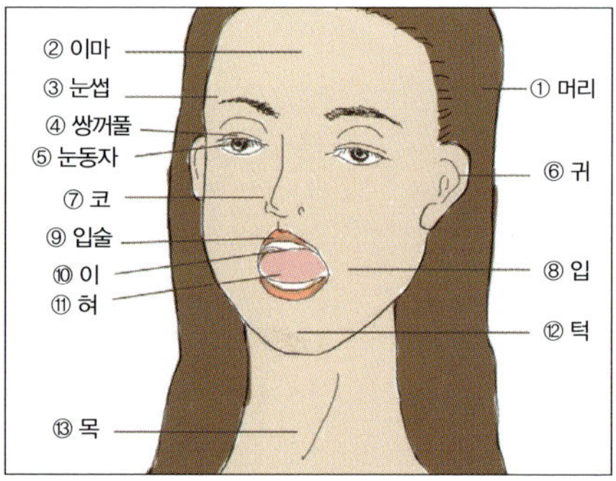

| 손 Hand |

① **손목** wrist

② **손등** back of the hand

③ **손가락** finger

④ **손바닥** palm

⑤ **주먹** fist

| 발 Foot |

① **발가락** toe ② **발꿈치** heel

③ **발바닥** sole

| 얼굴 Face |

① **머리** hair ② **이마** forehead

③ **눈썹** eyebrow ④ **쌍꺼풀** double eyelid

⑤ **눈동자** pupil ⑥ **귀** ear

⑦ **코** nose ⑧ **입** mouth

⑨ **입술** lip ⑩ **이** tooth

⑪ **혀** tongue ⑫ **턱** chin; jaw

⑬ **목** neck

R Synonyms

a little	좀, 조금
a while	잠깐, 잠시
all together	모두, 전부
beauty shop	미용실, 미장원
bookstore	서점, 책방
box	상자, 박스
car	자동차, 차
cell phone	휴대폰, 핸드폰, 휴대전화
country	나라, 국가
dance	무용, 춤
especially	특히, 특별히
everyday	날마다, 매일
extremely	매우, 굉장히
free of charge	공짜, 무료
habit	버릇, 습관
intersection	사거리, 네거리
later	이따가, 나중에
nearby	근처, 근방
opposite side	건너편, 맞은편, 반대편
reading books	독서, 책읽기
restaurant	식당, 음식점
road	도로, 길
store, shop	가게, 상점
straight	똑바로, 쭉
sun	해, 태양
the most	가장, 제일
this year	금년, 올해
to be comfortable	편하다, 편안하다
to be difficult	힘들다, 어렵다
to finish	마치다, 끝내다
to look for, search	찾다, 구하다
to mail, send	부치다, 보내다
to place an order	주문하다, 시키다
to spend time	지내다, 보내다
to use	쓰다, 이용하다, 사용하다
to want, wish	바라다, 원하다
very, much	매우, 굉장히, 대단히, 참, 아주, 정말
world	세계, 세상

S Antonyms

가깝다 to be close	↔	멀다 to be far
길다 to be long	↔	짧다 to be short
넓다 to be wide; spacious	↔	좁다 to be narrow
높다 to be high	↔	낮다 to be low
뜨겁다 to be hot	↔	차갑다 to be cold
마중 welcoming	↔	배웅 seeing off
맑다 to be clear	↔	흐리다 to be cloudy
매다 to tie	↔	풀다 to untie
물어보다 to ask	↔	대답하다 to answer
바쁘다 to be busy	↔	한가하다 to be free
빌리다 to borrow	↔	갚다 to pay back
빠르다 to be fast	↔	느리다 to be slow
사다 to buy	↔	팔다 to sell
살다 to live	↔	죽다 to die
시끄럽다 to be noisy	↔	조용하다 to be quiet
시작 beginning	↔	끝 end
싸다 to be cheap	↔	비싸다 to be expensive

S Antonyms

아까 a while ago	↔	이따가 later
아이 child	↔	어른 adult
알다 to know	↔	모르다 to no know
얇다 to be thin	↔	두껍다 to be thick
열다 to open	↔	닫다 to close
웃다 to laugh, smile	↔	울다 to cry
이기다 to win	↔	지다 to lose
입구 entrance	↔	출구 exit
입원 hospitalization	↔	퇴원 to be discharged from the hospital
입학 entrance into a school	↔	졸업 graduation
좋다 to be good	↔	나쁘다 to be bad
처음 the first	↔	마지막 the last
출발 departure	↔	도착 arrival
크다 to be big	↔	작다 to be small
타다 to ride	↔	내리다 to get off
편하다 to be comfortable	↔	불편하다 to be uncomfortable
필요하다 to be necessary	↔	필요없다 to be unnecessary

GLOSSARY

PC방 Internet café 15-7

가게 store, shop 1-1, 2-11

가깝다 to be close 2-1, 23-7

가끔 sometimes, once in a while, occasionally 3-1, 5-17

가르치다 to teach; to inform, tell 4-1, 22-8

가볍다 to be light 11-7

가운데 middle (place); center 5-1

가을 fall 20-1

가장 ad most, best 22-18

가족 family 6-1

가족 관계 family relations 6-1

간식 snack; food eaten between meals 7-1

감기 cold 8-1

강 river2-8

강의실 lecture room 4-2

같다 to be the same 9-1, 17-3

같이 together10-1, 18-5

갚다 to pay back 5-10

거스름돈 change (money) 23-4

거칠다 to be rough 11-9

건너편 the opposite side 11-1

건물 building 12-1

걷다 to walk 13-1

걸리다[1] to be caught 14-1

걸리다[2] to take time 15-1

걸어가다 to go on foot 13-1

걸어 다니다 to walk around, walk about 16-3

걸어오다 to come on foot 13-1

겨울 winter 20-1

결혼 marriage 16-1

결혼식 wedding ceremony 16-1

결혼하다 to get married 16-1

경제 economy 17-1

경제학 economics 17-1

경찰 the police; policeman 18-1

경찰관 police officer 18-1

경찰서 police station 18-1

계시다 to exist; to be at (honorific) 19-1, 24-15

계절 season (of a year) 20-1

계획 plan 21-1

계획하다 to plan 21-1

고객님 customer 6-12

고속도로 highway, freeway 18-4

고층 건물 high-rise building, skyscraper12-1

고향 hometown; home country; one's birth place 22-1

공원 park 23-1

공중 화장실 public restroom 16-20

공짜 free of charge 12-7

공항 airport 24-1

공항 버스 airport limousine bus 24-1

공휴일 legal holiday, bank holiday 21-20

과거 past 22-7

과목 course 10-12

과일 fruit 25-1

과일 가게 fruit store 25-1

괜찮다 to be okay 1-2

굉장하다 to be amazing, magnificent 2-2

굉장히 very; extremely 2-2, 7-4, 16-7, 18-6

교과서 textbook 3-2

교실 classroom 4-2

교통 traffic; transportation 5-2

교통 경찰 traffic police 5-2, 18-1

교통사고 traffic accident 5-2, 10-10

구경 looking around (with interest); sightseeing 6-2

구경하다 to look around with interest; to sightsee 6-2

구름 cloud 7-2, 23-20

구름이 끼다 to get cloudy 7-2

구하다 to look for, seek 4-19

국가 country, nation 24-2

국내선 domestic lines 24-1

국립 공원 national park 23-1
국제 공항 international airport 24-1
국제 무역 international trade14-7
국제선 international lines 24-1
귀여워하다 to love (on), adore 8-2
귀엽다 to be cute 8-2
그동안 meanwhile, during the time9-2, 5-5
그리다 to draw 10-2
그림 painting, drawing 10-2
극장 theater 11-2, 8-15
근방 nearby 12-2
근처 near place; vicinity12-2
금년 this year 13-2
금방 just now 16-8
기다리다 to wait for 14-2
기분 feeling 15-2
기쁘다 to be glad, happy 17-12
기숙사 dormitory 16-2
기차 train 17-2
기차역 train station 17-2, 20-17, 25-14
기차표 train ticket 3-20
길 street, road 18-4
길다 to be long 18-2, 23-18
깜짝 놀라다 to be startled all of a sudden 12-3
깨끗하다 to be clean 19-2, 13-4, 6-19
꽃 flower 20-2
꽃이 지다/시들다 (flower) to wither 20-2
꽃이 피다 (flower) to bloom 20-2
꽃집 flower shop 20-2
꿈 dream 21-2
꿈을 꾸다 to dream 21-2
끝 end 22-2, 24-11
끝나다 (event) to be over 22-2, 24-11
끝내다 to finish 8-6, 22-2
끼다 to put on (rings, gloves) 8-10
깨다 to wake (up) 17-16
나가다 to go out 23-2
나라 country, nation 24-2
나무 tree; wood 25-2
나쁘다 to be bad 1-3, 3-18
나오다 to come out 23-2
나이 age 2-3
나이가 많다 to be old 2-3, 19-14
나이가 적다/어리다 to be young 2-3
나중에 later 9-16, 22-6
날마다 ad every day 19-6
날씨 weather 3-3, 16-16
남자 배우 actor 21-8
낫다 to recover (from an illness) 14-1
낮다 to be low 4-3, 13-3
내년 next year 13-2
내다 to submit, turn in; to pay (money) 5-3
내리다 to get off (from transportation); to lower, go down 6-3, 19-19
너무 too much; very 7-3
넓다 to be wide; to be spacious 8-3, 25-17
넘어지다 to fall, trip over 22-5
넣다 to put in 9-3
네거리 intersection 9-10
노란색 yellow 4-11
노래 song 10-3
노래를 부르다 to sing a song 12-9
노래방 noraebang, karaoke 10-3, 15-7
놀다 to play; to hang out11-3
놀라다 to be surprised, startled; to be amazed 12-3
놀러 가다 to go to play, go on an excursion 11-3
놀러 다니다 to play about 16-3
놀러 오다 to come to play 11-3
높다 to be high 13-3, 4-3
놓다 1. to lay, put something down 2. to release, let go 14-3
눕다 to lie down 9-11, 13-14
느리다 to be slow 6-10

GLOSSARY

늦게 late 15-3
늦다 to be delayed; to be late 15-3
다니다 to go (and attend) regularly 16-3
다르다 to be different 17-3, 9-1
다름이 아니라 It is just that... 17-3
다리 bridge 18-3
다시 again, once more 19-3
다음 next, following 20-3, 15-18
다음 달 next month 20-3
다음 주 next week 20-3, 9-18
다음 해 next year 20-3
다치다 to get hurt, be injured 21-3
닦다 to clean, wipe, wash, polish 22-3
닫다 to close, shut 23-3, 6-15
닫히다 to be closed (passive form of 닫다) 23-3
달 the moon 10-20
달다 to taste sweet 24-3, 20-6
달력 calendar 25-3
달리기 running 1-4
달리다 to run, dash 1-4, 13-1, 24-5
닮다 to resemble, take after, look alike 2-4
담그다 to soak, put something in liquid; to make (kimchi) 3-4
담배 cigarette 4-4
답 answer 5-4
답장 reply letter 6-4
답하다 to answer (=대답하다) 5-4
대단하다 to be huge, enormous, great 7-4
대단히 ad greatly, extremely 2-2
대단히 very much; extremely 7-4, 18-6
대답하다 to answer, give a reply 8-4, 19-7
대도시 large city 20-4
대부분 most part of something; mostly 9-4
대중 목욕탕 public bath house 9-7
대중교통 public transportation 5-2
대통령 president of a country 10-4
대화 conversation, dialogue 11-4
대화를 나누다 to have a conversation 11-4
대화하다 to converse 11-4
대회 big event, conference; (sport) competition, championship, contest 12-4
더 more 15-4
더럽다 to be dirty 13-4, 19-2
덕분 favor 14-4
덜 less; incompletely 15-4
덥다 (weather) to be hot 16-4, 9-19, 23-13
덮다 to cover 17-4
도로 road, street 18-4
도서관 library 19-4
도시 city 20-4, 9-12, 20-12
도와 드리다 to help (a respectable person) 8-5
도와주다 to give/lend help 2-5
도움 help 2-5
도착 arrival 21-4
도착 시간 arrival time 21-4
도착하다 to arrive at 21-4
독서 reading books 22-4
독서하다 to read books 22-4
돈 money 23-4
돈을 내다 to pay money 23-4, 5-3
돈을 모으다 to save money 7-7
돈을 벌다 to make or earn money 23-4
돈을 부치다 to remit (send) money 17-9
돈을 빌리다 to borrow money 23-4
돈을 쓰다 to spend money 23-4
돈을 찾다 to withdraw money (from the bank) 23-4
돌 one's first birthday 24-4
돌다 to turn 25-4
돌려 드리다 to return (something to an honorable person) 1-5
돌려주다 to return (something) 1-5
돌아가시다 to die, pass away 25-4, 10-18
돌잔치 the birthday party for one's one-year-old baby 24-4

돕다 to help 2-5
동네 village, town; neighborhood area 3-5
동네 사람 neighborhood people (=이웃) 3-5
동물 animal 4-5
동물원 zoo 4-5
동안 during, for (time period) 5-5, 9-2
두껍다 to be thick 6-5
두다 to put, place, leave 7-5
드리다 to give (humble) 8-5, 4-18
드시다 to eat (honorific form of 먹다) 9-5
듣다 to listen; to take a course 10-5
들다[1] to lift up, raise11-5
들다[2] to cost money; take time 12-5
들리다 to be heard, be audible 13-5
들어가다 to enter; to go in 14-5
들어오다 to come in 14-5
등산 hiking, mountain climbing 23-5, 22-10
등산객 mountain climber 23-5
등산하다 to hike, climb mountain 23-5
따뜻하다 to be mild, warm; to be kind 16-5, 23-13
따라 하다 to repeat after; to imitate what other person does 17-5
따라가다 to follow; to go after 17-5
따라오다 to follow; to come with 17-5
따로 separately; additionally 18-5
따르다 to follow 17-5
딱딱하다 to be hard 11-9
땀 sweat 19-5
땀을 흘리다 to (shed) sweat 19-5
땀이 나다 to sweat 19-5
떠나다 to leave 20-5
떠들다 to chat, make a noise 21-5
떨어지다 to fall, drop 22-5
똑같다 to be exactly the same 2-10, 9-1, 17-3
똑바로 straight, upright correctly 23-6, 24-17
뛰다 to run, dash; to jump 24-5, 1-4, 13-1
뜨겁다 to be hot, burning25-5
뜻 meaning, sense 1-6
마르다[1] to dry up 2-6
마르다[2] to lose weight; to become thin, skinny, slim 21-6
마시다 to drink 4-6, 3-6
마음 heart, nature 5-6
마음에 들다 to be in one's like 5-6
마중 welcoming a person, reception 6-6
마지막 the last 7-6, 5-19
마지막으로 finally, lastly 7-6
마치다 to finish, complete 8-6
마침표 period mark 8-6
막히다 to be blocked, congested 9-6
만나다 to meet 10-6
만남 meeting 10-6
만들다 to make 11-6
만지다 to touch, pet, feel 12-6
많다 to be many, much 13-6, 15-17
말 words, speech 14-6
말다 to stop, cease; not ... but ...15-5
말하다 to speak 12-16, 14-6
맑다 to be clear, pure 16-6, 23-20
맞다 to be correct, right; to fit, suit 17-6
맞은편 the opposite side 11-1
매 학기 every semester 19-6
매년 every year 19-6
매다 to tie 4-20
매달 every month 19-6
매번 every time 19-6
매시간 every hour 19-6
매우 very much, extremely 18-6, 2-2, 16-7
매월 every month 19-6
매일 every day 19-6
매주 every week 19-6
맵다 to taste spicy, hot 20-6, 17-13, 24-3
머리 모양 hair style 6-7

GLOSSARY

먹다 to eat (food); to drink (liquid); to take (medicine) 3-6

먼저 in advance, first, earlier 22-6

멀다 to be far 23-7, 2-1

멋있다 to be stylish, cool, fashionable 24-6

메다 to carry something on one's shoulder 25-6

며칠 what day of the month; a few days 1-7

면도 shaving 2-7

면도기 razor 2-7

면도하다 to shave 2-7

모두 all, all together 3-7

모르다 to not know, be unaware of, not understand 4-7, 15-14

모시다 to take (escort) someone (older) 5-7

모양 shape, form 6-7

모으다 to gather; to collect, accumulate 7-7, 8-7

모이다 to get together 8-7

모임 gathering 8-7

목감기 sore throat 8-1

목소리 voice 1-12

목욕탕 bathroom 9-7

목욕하다 to take a bath 9-7, 22-11

몸이 안 좋다 15-2

못생기다 to be ugly 6-11, 8-17

못하다 to be unable to do; cannot do 10-7

무겁다 to be heavy 11-7

무료 free of charge 12-7

무료로 for free 12-7

무섭다 to be scary; to be scared of 13-7

무역 trade 14-7

무용 (classical) dance, dancing 15-6

무척 very, really, extremely 16-7

문제 question, problem 17-7

문화 culture 18-7

묻다 to ask 19-7

물건 thing; item; product 20-7

물론 (being) needless to say 21-7

물어보다 to ask 8-4, 22-19

미래 future 22-7

미리 in advance, ahead of time 23-8

미술관 art museum 8-8

미용실 beauty shop, hairdresser's 24-7, 10-16

미장원 beauty shop 24-7, 10-16

밀리다 to be left undone 25-7

바꾸다 to switch, change 1-8

바뀌다 to be changed 1-8

바다 sea, ocean 2-8

바닷가 sea side, beach 2-8

바라다 to wish, want, hope 3-8

바람 wind; air 4-8

바로 right (there), directly 5-8

바르다 to apply, spread 6-8

바쁘다 to be busy 7-8

박물관 museum 8-8

박수 handclap, applause 9-8

박스 box 25-10

반대편 the opposite side 11-1

반찬 side dish 10-8

받다 to receive, get, accept 11-8

발음 pronunciation 12-8

발음하다 to pronounce 12-8

발표 presentation, announcement 13-8

발표하다 to announce, make a presentation 13-8

밝다 to be bright 14-8

밥 cooked rice 6-13

밥상 (Korean style) dining table 7-13

방 room 15-7

방금 just now 16-8

방법 way, means, method 17-8

방송 broadcasting 18-8

방송국 broadcasting station 18-8

방송되다 to be broadcast 18-8

방송하다 to broadcast 18-8
방학 school vacation, break 19-8
배가 고프다 to be hungry 13-9
배달 delivery 20-8
배우 actor, actress 21-8
배우다 to learn, take lessons 22-8, 4-1
배웅하다 to see somebody off 6-6
백화점 department store 23-9
버릇 habit 18-12
버리다 to throw away 23-10
버스 정류장 bus stop 20-17, 25-14
벌써 already 25-8, 7-14
벽 wall 1-9
벽시계 wall clock 1-9
별 star 2-9
별로 (not) really, (not) particularly 3-9
병 sickness, illness 4-9
병에 걸리다 to get sick 4-9
병원 hospital 4-9
병이 낫다 to get well, to be healed 4-9
보내다 to pass, to send (mail, text or money); to spend (time) 5-9, 16-18
보통 average; usually, commonly 6-9, 5-18
복도 hallway 7-9
복잡하다 to be crowded; to be complicated 8-9
볶다 to stir fry, roast 9-9
볶음밥 fried rice 9-9
봄 spring 20-1
봉투 envelope; bag (for grocery or garbage) 10-9
부드럽다 to be soft, tender, smooth 11-9
부르다[1] to call (out a person) 12-9
부르다[2] to be bulged out, full 13-9
부모 parents 14-9
부부 married couple, husband and wife 15-8
부지런하다 to be hard working, diligent 16-9
부치다 to send (a letter or money) 17-9
부탁 favor, request 18-9
부탁을 들어주다 to do a favor for somebody 18-9
부탁하다 to ask a favor 18-9
분위기 atmosphere, ambience, mood, air 19-9
불다 to blow; to play wind instruments 20-9
불친절하다 to be unkind, unfriendly 13-19
불편하다 to be uncomfortable, inconvenient 21-9, 1-20, 24-18
불행 misfortune, unhappiness 11-20
붓다[1] to swell, become swollen 22-9
붓다[2] to pour, put (liquid) 23-11
붙다 to stick to, adhere to; to pass (an exam) 24-8
붙이다 to stick, attach, glue 25-9, 24-8
비밀 secret 1-10
비슷하다 to be similar, alike 2-10
비싸다 to be expensive 3-10, 18-13
비자 visa 23-14
비행기 airplane 4-10
비행기 표 airplane ticket 3-20
빌려주다 to lend, rent 5-10
빌리다 to borrow 5-10
빠르다 to be fast 6-10
빨간색 red 4-11
빨다 to wash clothes 7-10
빨래 laundry 7-10, 24-10
빨래방 laundromat 7-10, 15-7
빨래하다 to do the laundry 7-10
빨리 quickly 6-10
빼다 to take off (accessories or gloves); to pull out; to subtract 8-10
사거리 intersection 9-10
사계절 four seasons 20-1
사고 accident 10-10
사귀다 to make friends with someone; to date someone 11-10
사다 to buy 12-10, 23-19
사랑 love 13-10

GLOSSARY

사랑하다 to love 13-10
사무실 office (room) 14-10, 1-15
사업 business 15-9
사업가 business man 15-9
사업하다 to do business 15-9
사용하다 to use, make use of 16-10, 24-12
사이 gap or space (between); (personal) relationship 17-10
사장 president of a company, CEO 18-10
사전 dictionary 19-10
사진 picture, photograph 20-10
사촌 cousin 21-10
산 mountain 22-10, 2-8
산꼭대기 top of a mountain 22-10
산책 walk, stroll 15-10
산책로 trail 15-10
산책하다 to take a walk 15-10
살다 to live 24-9, 10-18
삼거리 three-way intersection 9-10
삼촌 uncle 21-10
상자 box 25-10
상점 store, shop 2-11, 1-1
상처 injury, wound, cut 1-11, 21-3
상처를 입다 to get hurt 21-3
새 new 3-11
새로 newly 3-11
색 color 4-11
색깔 color 4-11
생각 thought, thinking, idea 5-11
생각하다 to think 5-11
생기다 to get, obtain something; to happen; to appear, look 6-11
생신 birthday (honorific) 7-11
생일 birthday 7-11
생활 life, living 8-11
생활비 the cost of living 8-11
서다 to stand; to stop, halt 9-11, 13-14, 23-12
서로 each other, one another 10-11
서류 document 11-11
서울역 Seoul Station 25-14
서점 bookstore 12-11
선물 gift, present 13-11
선물 가게 gift shop 1-1, 13-11
선배 a senior member at school or work place 14-11
선수 athlete, player 15-11
선택 choice 16-11
선택하다 to choose 16-11
설거지 dishwashing 17-11
설거지하다 to wash dishes 17-11
설명하다 to explain 18-11
성 family name 19-11
성격 personality 20-11
성적 grade 18-17
성함 (full) name (honorific) 19-11
세계 the world 21-11
세계 지도 world map 18-18
세계적인 world famous 21-11
세발 자전거 tricycle 4-17
세상 the world, society 21-11
세수 washing one's face 22-11
세수하다 to wash one's face 22-11
세우다 to stop; to park (a vehicle); to make someone/ something stop 23-12
세탁 washing clothes 24-10
세탁기 washing machine 7-10, 24-10
세탁소 dry cleaner's 24-10
세탁하다 to wash clothes 24-10
소개 introduction 25-11
소개하다 to introduce 25-11
소리 sound 1-12
소리를 지르다 to scream, shout 1-12
소설 novel, fiction 2-12
소설가 novelist 2-12

소식 news 3-12
소포 package, parcel (as a type of mail) 4-12
소풍 picnic, excursion 5-12
소풍 가다 to go on a picnic 5-12
손님 guest, customer 6-12
손뼉 clap 9-8
손수건 handkerchief 7-12
수고하다 to make an effort, to take the trouble 8-12
수도 capital city of a country 9-12, 20-4
수업 class 10-12
수저 spoons and chopsticks; spoon 11-12, 13-12
숙제 homework; assignment 12-12
숟가락 spoon 13-12, 11-12
숫자 number 14-12
쉬다 to take a rest; to take a day off 15-12
쉽다 to be easy 16-12, 18-14
스마트폰 smart phone 17-17
슬프다 to be sad 17-12
습관 habit 18-12
시 poetry, poem 2-12
시간 time; hours (counter for duration) 19-12
시골 the countryside, rural area 20-12
시끄럽다 to be noisy 21-12, 24-16
시내 downtown, intra-city 22-12
시내 버스 intra-city bus 22-12
시다 to be sour 20-6, 24-3
시원하다 to be cool; to be refreshing 23-13
시작 beginning, start 24-11, 22-2
시작하다 to begin, start 24-11, 8-6
시장 market, marketplace 25-12
시청 city hall 1-13
시키다 to order (food in a restaurant); to make someone do something 2-13, 7-18
시험 test, exam 3-13
시험을 보다 to take an exam 3-13
식구 family 6-1
식다 to cool off, get cold 4-13
식당 restaurant 5-13
식사 meal; having a meal 6-13
식사하다 to have a meal 6-13
식사하시다 to have a meal (honorific) 9-5
식탁 dining table 7-13
신기하다 to be amazing, wonderful; novel, new 8-13
신나다 to be excited, to be exciting 9-13
신문 newspaper 10-13, 12-17
신문지 newspaper (refers to the physical paper) 10-13
신발 가게 shoe store 1-1
신용카드 credit card 12-20
신청 application; request; sign-up 11-13
신청서 application 11-13
신청하다 to apply; to sign up 11-13
신호등 traffic light 12-13
신혼부부 newly married couple 15-8
실수 mistake 13-13
실수로 by mistake 13-13
실수하다 to make a mistake 13-13
실험실 laboratory, lab 1-15
싫다 to be unpleasant; not likable 14-13, 3-18
싫어하다 to dislike 3-18, 14-13
심심하다 to be bored (because there is nothing interesting to do) 15-13
심하다 to be serious, severe, harsh 16-13
싱겁다 to taste bland 17-13, 20-6
싸다 to be cheap 18-13, 3-10
싸우다 to fight, argue 19-13
쌀쌀하다 (weather) to be cold, chilly 16-5
쌓이다 to get stacked, increase 20-13
썰다 to cut, slice, chop (usually with a knife) 21-13
쓰기 writing 22-13
쓰다 to be bitter 20-6, 24-3

GLOSSARY

쓰다[1] to write 22-13

쓰다[2] to use 24-12, 16-10

쓰레기 trash, garbage 24-19

쓰레기 봉투 garbage bag 10-9

쓰레기 trash, waste 22-14

쓰레기통 trash can 22-14

씹다 to chew 25-13

씻다 to wash 1-14, 22-3

아까 a while ago 2-14, 16-8

아름답다 to be beautiful 3-14, 9-15

아마 probably, perhaps 4-14

아이 child 5-14, 20-14

아주 very (much), so, really; extremely; completely 6-14, 21-17

아직 still, yet 7-14, 25-8

아침 morning/breakfast 19-17

아프다 to be sick; painful 8-14

악기 musical instrument 9-14

악기를 연주하다 to play/perform on instruments 9-14

안녕하다 to be well; feel well 10-14

안녕히 well 10-14

안다 to hold, hug 11-14

안부 regards, news on whether someone is fine 12-14

앉다 to sit 13-14, 9-11

않다 to not be, to not do 14-14

알다 to know 15-14, 4-7

애완 동물 pet 4-5

야채 vegetable 25-1

약 medicine 16-14

약국 pharmacy 16-4

약도 rough map (for a direction) 18-18

약사 pharmacist 16-4

약속 promise 17-14, 10-15

약속을 지키다 to keep one's promise 17-14

약속하다 to make a promise 17-14

약혼하다 to be engaged

얇다 to be thin 6-5

양치질하다 to brush one's teeth 22-11

어둡다 to be dark 14-8

어렵다 to be difficult, hard 18-14, 16-13, 25-20

어른 adult, (one's) elders 20-14, 5-14

어리다 to be young 19-14

어린이 child 19-14, 20-14

어울리다 to fit, go along well; to socialize 21-14

얼다 to freeze 22-15

얼음 ice 22-15

여권 passport 23-14

여름 summer 20-1

여름 방학 summer vacation 19-8

여배우 actress 21-8

여행 travel, trip 24-13

여행사 travel agency 24-13

여행하다 to travel 24-13

역 (train or subway) station 25-14

연구실 professor's office; laboratory 1-15, 14-10

연락 contact 2-15

연락처 contact information (e.g. phone number, e-mail address) 2-15

연락하다 to contact 2-15

연습 exercise, practice 3-15

연습 문제 exercises, exercise questions 3-15

연습실 practice room 3-15

연습하다 to practice 3-15

연주 musical performance 4-15

연주하다 to play (musical instruments) 4-15

열 fever, heat 5-15

열다 to open 6-15, 23-3

열심히 hard, diligently 7-15

열이 나다 to run a fever 5-15

영화 movie 8-15

영화배우 movie actor/actress 8-15

영화관 movie theater 8-15, 11-2

영화를 보다 to watch a movie 8-15

영화표 movie ticket 8-15
예쁘다 to be pretty, beautiful 9-15
예약 reservation, appointment 10-15
예약하다 to make a reservation/appointment 10-15
옛날 long time ago 11-15
오래 for a long while 12-15
오래간만 after a long while (=오랜만) 12-15
오랫동안 for a long time 5-5, 12-15
오르다 to climb, increase 13-15
올해 this year 13-2
옷 가게 clothing store 1-1
외국 foreign country 14-15
외국어 foreign language 14-15
외국인 foreigner 14-15
외사촌 cousin on the mother's side 21-10
외식하다 to eat out 15-15
외출하다 to go out 16-15
요금 fee, fare 17-15
요리 cooking 18-15
요리사 chef, cook 18-15
요리하다 to cook 18-15
요즘 these days, nowadays 19-15
우리 나라 my country 24-2
우산 umbrella 20-15
우체국 post office 21-15
우체부 mailman 21-15
우체통 mailbox 21-15
운동 sports, exercise 22-16
운동 선수 sport player 15-11, 22-16
운동복 sportswear 22-16
운동장 playground 22-16
운동하다 to do exercises 22-16
운동화 sneakers 22-16
운전 driving 23-15
운전 기사 driver 23-15
운전 면허 driver's license 23-15
운전하다 to drive 23-15
울다 to cry 24-14, 25-15
울음 crying 24-14
웃다 to laugh, smile 25-15, 24-14
웃음 laughter 25-15
원하다 to want 3-8
웬일 what matter...? what reason...? 1-16
유명하다 to be famous 2-16
유행 fashion, trend 3-16
유행하다 to be in trend 3-16
은행 bank 4-16
은행원 banker 4-16
음료수 beverage 5-16
음식 food 6-16
음식을 만들다 to prepare food, to cook 6-16
음식점 restaurant 5-13, 6-16
음악 music 7-16
음악가 musician 7-16
음악을 듣다 to listen to music 7-16
음악회 musical concert 7-16
이기다 to win, beat 8-16, 17-18
이따(가) little later 9-16, 22-6, 2-14
이름 (first) name 19-11
이메일 email 6-4
이발소 barber shop 10-16, 24-7
이번 주(일) this week 9-18
이사 moving (of one's residence) 11-16
이사하다 to move 11-16
이삿짐센터 moving company 11-16
이야기하다 to talk, chat 12-16
이용하다 to make use of 16-10, 24-12
이혼 divorce 16-1
인사 greeting, salutation, bow 13-16
인사하다 to greet, give a bow 13-16
일 work 14-16
일기 journal, diary 15-16
일기예보 weather forecast 16-16, 3-3

GLOSSARY

일어나다 to get up 17-16
일찍 early 18-16
일하다 to work 14-16
읽다 to read (something) 19-16
잃다 to lose 20-16
입구 entrance 21-16
입원하다 to be hospitalized 22-17
입학 admission to a school 23-16
입학하다 to be admitted to a school 23-16
있다 to be, exist; to have, possess 24-15
잊다 to forget 25-16
잊어버리다 25-16
자기소개 self-introduction 25-11
자다 to sleep 1-17
자동차 car, automobile 2-17
자라다 to grow up 3-17, 20-19
자르다 to cut, slice 21-13
자전거 bicycle 4-17
자주 frequently, often 5-17, 3-1
작년 last year 13-2
작다 to be small 6-17, 15-17, 17-19
잘 못하다 to be not very good at something 9-17
잘못 wrong; anything done wrong 7-17
잘못하다 to make a mistake 7-17
잘생기다 to be handsome 8-17, 6-11
잘하다 to do well 9-17
잠 sleep 1-17
잠(을) 자다 to sleep 1-17
잠깐 short time; for a moment, briefly 10-17
잠깐 동안 for a short time 5-5
잠시 for a moment 10-17
잠이 들다 to fall asleep 1-17
잠이 오다 to get sleepy 1-17
잡다 to catch, grab 11-17
잡지 magazine, journal 12-17
장소 location 13-17
재미없다 to be no fun, to be boring 14-17
재미있다 to be fun 14-17
저녁 evening/dinner 19-17
적다 (amount) **to be few, little 15-17**, 13-6
적어도 at least 15-17
전공 major 16-17
전공하다 to major in 16-17
전부 all, the entire 3-7
전화 phone call, telephone 17-17
전화기 telephone set 17-17
전화번호 telephone number 17-17
전화비 telephone bill 17-17
전화하다to make a call (= 전화를 걸다) 17-17
절 (Korean style formal) bow 13-16
절하다 to bow 13-16
점수 score, point 18-17
점심 lunch 19-17
점심 시간 lunch time 19-17
젓가락 chopsticks 11-12, 13-12
정도 about, around 25-18
정류장 (bus) stop 20-17
정말 really; real story 21-17, 6-14
정상 top of a mountain 2-10
제일 the first, the most 22-18
조금 little 23-17
조용하다 to be quiet, silent 24-16, 21-12
졸업 graduation 23-16
좀 a little; please 23-17
좁다 to be narrow 25-17, 8-3
종업원 waiter, waitress; employee 1-18
종이 (a piece of) paper 2-18
좋다 to be good 3-18, 1-3, 14-13
좋아하다 to like 3-18
주 a week 9-18
주다 to give 4-18, 11-8
주로 mainly, mostly, usually 5-18
주말 weekend 6-18, 2-20
주무시다 to sleep (honorific) 1-17

주문하다 to order 7-18, 2-13
주소 address 8-18
주일 a week 9-18
주 중 weekday 2-20, 6-18
죽다 to die 10-18, 24-9
준비 preparation 11-18
준비하다 to prepare 11-18
줄을 서다 to stay in line 9-11
중소 도시 mid-sized and small cities 20-4
중요하다 to be important, significant 12-18
즐겁다 to be pleasant, joyful 13-18, 17-12
지금 now 14-18
지나다 to pass, go by 15-18
지난 last 15-18, 20-3
지난 달 last month 15-18
지난 번 last time 15-18
지난 주 last week 15-18
지내다 to spend (one's) time; to get along 16-18, 5-9
지다 to be defeated; to lose 17-18, 8-16
지도 map 18-18
지하 underground, below 19-18
지하도 underpass 19-18
지하실 basement 19-18
지하철 subway 19-18
지하철역 subway station 19-18, 20-17, 25-14
직업 occupation, career, job 20-18
직장 workplace 20-18
직접 directly, in person, personally 21-18
진공 청소기 vacuum cleaner 6-19
질문 question 22-19, 5-4
짜다 to be salty 17-13, 20-6, 24-3
짧다 to be short 23-18, 18-2
쭉 straight; all the time 24-17, 23-6
쯤 about, around 25-18
찍다 to take (a photograph), film (a video/movie) 1-19
찜질방 Korean dry sauna 15-7
차 car 2-17
차갑다 to be cold 25-5
차다 to kick 2-19
착하다 to be nice, good-natured 3-19
참 truly, really 6-14, 21-17
찾다 to look for, find, search; to withdraw money (from the bank or ATM) 4-19
채소 vegetable 25-1
책방 book store 12-11
책읽기 reading books 22-4
처음 the beginning, the first time 5-19, 7-6
처음으로 for the first time 5-19
청소 cleaning-up 6-19
청소하다 to clean up 6-19
축하하다 to congratulate 7-19
출구 exit 21-16
출발 departure 21-4
춤 dance 8-19, 15-6
춤을 추다 to dance 8-19
춥다 to be cold 9-19, 16-4
취미 hobby; interest 10-19
치다 to play (tennis, piano, guitar); to hit 11-19
친구 friend 12-19
친절하다 to be kind, friendly, considerate 13-19, 14-19
친하다 to be close, intimate 14-19
침대 bed 15-19
칼 knife, sword 16-19
코감기 sinus cold 8-1
크기 size 17-19
크다 to be big 17-19, 6-17
키 height 18-19
키가 작다 to be short 18-19
키가 크다 to be tall 18-19
타다 to get in (on); to ride 19-19, 6-3
태양 the sun 10-20

GLOSSARY

태어나다 to be born 20-19

통화 phone call 21-19

통화하다 to talk over the phone 21-19

퇴원하다 to be discharged from the hospital 22-17

튀기다 to deep-fry 9-9

특별히 particularly, especially 22-20

특히 particularly, especially 22-20

틀리다 to be incorrect, wrong 17-6

파란색 blue 4-11

팔다 to sell 23-19, 12-10

편리하다 to be convenient 24-18, 1-20, 21-9

편안하다 to be comfortable 1-20

편지 letter 25-19, 6-4

편지를 부치다 to send a letter 17-9

편지봉투 letter envelope 10-9

편하다 to be comfortable; to feel easy 1-20, 21-9, 24-18

평일 weekday 2-20, 6-18

표 ticket 3-20

풀다 to take off (tie, belt, watch); to solve a problem 4-20

피곤하다 to be tired, exhausted 5-20

필요없다 to be not necessary 6-20

필요하다 to be needed, necessary 6-20

하늘 sky 7-20

하늘색 sky blue 4-11, 7-20

학기 semester, academic term 8-20

학점 credit, grade 18-17

한가운데 right in the middle 5-1

한가하다 to be free 7-8

한자 Chinese character 9-20

항공기 air craft 4-10

항상 all the time 5-18

해 the sun 10-20

핸드폰 cell phone 20-20

햇빛 sunlight, sunshine 10-20, 23-20

행복 happiness 11-20

행복하다 to be happy 11-20

헤어지다 to part, break up10-6

현금 cash 12-20

현재 present 22-7

호수 lake 2-8

혼자 alone 13-20

화 anger, rage 14-20

화가 나다 to be angry 14-20

화장 make-up 15-20

화장실 restroom 16-20, 9-7

화장품 cosmetics 15-20

화장품 가게 cosmetics store 1-1

화장하다 to wear makeup 15-20

회사 company 17-20

회사원 employee, worker 17-20

회의 meeting, conference 18-20

회의실 meeting room 18-20

회의하다 to have a meeting 18-20

횡단보도 crosswalk 19-20

후배 a junior member at school or work place 14-11

휴대전화 mobile phone, cellular phone 20-20, 17-17

휴대폰 cell phone 20-20

휴일 holiday, day off 21-20

휴지 wastepaper, garbage (paper); tissue, toilet paper 24-19, 22-14

휴지통 trash can 24-19

흐려지다 to become cloudy 23-20

흐리다 to be cloudy; to be unclear; to be overcast 23-20, 7-2, 16-6

힘 strength, energy, force 24-20, 25-20

힘들다 to be hard, tough, laborious; to be difficult 25-20, 24-20

힘이 세다 to be strong 24-20